Midwest Living®

TASTE OF THE SEASONS

Meredith® Consumer Marketing
Des Moines, Iowa

Midwest Living® Taste of the Seasons

Meredith® Corporation Consumer Marketing
VICE PRESIDENT, CONSUMER MARKETING: Janet Donnelly
CONSUMER MARKETING PRODUCT DIRECTOR: Heather Sorensen
BUSINESS DIRECTOR: Ron Clingman
CONSUMER MARKETING PRODUCT MANAGER: Wendy Merical
SENIOR PRODUCTION MANAGER: Al Rodruck

Waterbury Publications, Inc.
EDITORIAL DIRECTOR: Lisa Kingsley
ASSOCIATE EDITORS: Tricia Bergman, Mary Williams
CREATIVE DIRECTOR: Ken Carlson
ASSOCIATE DESIGN DIRECTOR: Doug Samuelson
PRODUCTION ASSISTANT: Mindy Samuelson
CONTRIBUTING COPY EDITOR: Gretchen Kauffman
CONTRIBUTING INDEXER: Elizabeth T. Parson

Midwest Living® **Magazine**
EDITOR IN CHIEF: Greg Philby
CREATIVE DIRECTOR: Geri Wolfe Boesen
EXECUTIVE EDITOR: Trevor Meers
FOOD EDITOR: Hannah Agran
COPY CHIEF: Maria Duryée

Meredith National Media Group
PRESIDENT: Tom Harty

Meredith Corporation
PRESIDENT AND CHIEF EXECUTIVE OFFICER: Stephen M. Lacy

IN MEMORIAM: E.T. Meredith III (1933–2003)

Pictured on the front cover:
Caramel Pecan Skillet Brownie
(recipe on page 174)
Photographer: Blaine Moats

Contents

The Art of Enjoying Food

ONCE, I WAS SO SMITTEN WITH A FORKFUL OF FILET MIGNON that, for a moment, I forgot the names of my dinner companions. Actually, I forgot they were even there. So mesmerized by the flavor, I only wanted to concentrate on it, to slow-chew with my eyes closed. My friends, the white tablecloth, the sparkling wine glasses, the salad—all washed away by my momentary culinary bliss.

This set off a discussion on food: Is it personal pleasure or shared enjoyment? We asked the chef his thoughts.

"Ah," he said. "Food is a social thing. It is to be shared with friends and family. Food is a celebration, like you're doing now." He bowed graciously, asked if we might like another bottle of wine perhaps and slipped away.

Food has powerful social impact. A Cider-Brined Turkey and Apples (page 195) served at the holiday table tastes of family tradition. A signature cake made by a mother or an aunt has a lifetime of memories stirred into it. An evening of warm conversation with friends is enjoyed over Cajun-Rubbed Salmon (page 145).

But I've also experienced a day on my own in Sault Ste. Marie, Michigan, savoring a local dairy's ice cream so flavorful it sweetened the world around me beyond the harbor of ships as though there was no end. I just felt happy.

There was the sautéing of morels in an old pan, just me and the dog one spring, in a cabin in the woods that smelled of ancient roots and fresh chances.

Another year, it was the apple that I twisted from a tree branch, laden with all the sensations—sweet, sour, tart, crisp, juicy—at the same time. It was like all of summer flowing from one sun-warmed bite.

Food creates bonds and makes memories. This book holds the year's best recipes, tested in our Test Kitchen to ensure they are easy, reliable and taste great.

Enjoy them with a group of family or friends. Savor a bite as a personal escape. Either way, they make life delicious.

Greg Philby
Editor in Chief

PEACH CORDIAL
MINI BUNDT CAKES,
PAGE 52

Spring

APPETIZERS & BEVERAGES

Cheese and Almond Guacamole 11

Lemonade Tea Punch 8

Mini Party Quiches 11

Ricotta and Parmesan Spread 8

BREADS

Apricot-Raisin Hot Cross Buns 15

Double-Strawberry Scones 12

Grilled Onion Flatbread with Bacon and Arugula 12

Hearty Waffles 15

MAIN DISHES

Asparagus-Tuna Casserole 33

Crispy Honey-Mustard Pork Chops 23

Garden Veggie Linguine with Cilantro Pesto 34

Greens, Egg and Ham Loaf 24

Grilled Steak 19

Herbed Chicken with Spring Vegetables 29

Italian Dinner Soup 27

Meat and Potato Pizza 27

Spinach-Mushroom-Sausage Pierogi Bake 30

Steak Sandwiches 20

Walleye Wild Rice Cakes with Wasabi Dressing 33

The White Burger 30

SAUCES & DRESSINGS

Asian Vinaigrette 40

Buttermilk Pesto Dressing 40

Chimichurri Sauce 19

Mole BBQ Sauce 19

Peanut Butter Dressing 39

Quick Dill Sauce 24

Strawberry Balsamic Dressing 40

Summer Hollandaise 43

Sweet Beet Chutney 23

Wasabi Dressing 33

SIDES

Asian Cabbage Salad 39

Grilled Vegetables 43

Herbed Potato Salad 43

Roasted Asparagus-Orange Salad 34

Strawberry and Arugula Salad with Manchego Fricos 39

SWEETS

Best-Ever Strawberry-Rhubarb Pie 49

Blueberry Cheesecake Cupcakes 50

Chai-Spiced Compote 44

Chocolate-Marshmallow Ice Cream Sandwiches 46

Choose-a-Fruit Fool 46

Gooey Butter Bars 55

Green Tea Ice Cream 45

Malt Shop Special Cupcakes 50

Peach Cordial Mini Bundt Cakes 52

Raspberry and Vanilla Stack Cakes 55

Rhubarb Fool 46

Root Beer Float Cupcakes 52

Salted Caramel, Chocolate and Peanut Cracker-Stack Bars 56

Vanilla Flan with Butterscotch Sauce 45

Lemonade Tea Punch

Indian Darjeeling tea has floral notes beyond what you find in ordinary black tea, making it a more interesting base for our refreshing, honey-laced punch.

PREP 15 minutes **STAND** 10 minutes
COOL 30 minutes **CHILL** 4 hours

    4 cups water
    3 inches fresh ginger, thinly sliced
   ¼ cup loose-leaf Darjeeling tea or other
       loose-leaf black tea
   ½ of a 12-ounce can (¾ cup) frozen
       lemonade concentrate, thawed
   ⅓ cup honey
       Ice cubes or crushed ice
       Lemon slices or thin lemon wedges

1. In a saucepan, bring the water and ginger to boiling. Remove from heat. Add tea. Let stand, covered, for 10 minutes. Pour tea mixture through a fine-mesh strainer. Discard ginger and tea leaves.

2. Transfer tea to a 1½-quart pitcher. Stir in lemonade concentrate and honey. Cool for 30 minutes. Chill, covered, for 4 hours or up to 24 hours.

3. Serve chilled punch in glasses over ice. Garnish with lemon slices. **Makes 6 servings.**

Per 6 ounces: 132 cal, 0 g fat, 0 mg chol, 9 mg sodium, 36 g carbo, 1 g fiber, 0 g pro.

Ricotta and Parmesan Spread

Be sure to use whole-milk ricotta for the best texture in this quick spread from BelGioioso Cheese in Wisconsin.

PREP 5 minutes **CHILL** 1 hour **BAKE** 8 minutes

    1 15- or 16-ounce container whole-milk
       ricotta cheese
    3 ounces Parmesan cheese, finely shredded
       (¾ cup)
   ¼ cup snipped fresh basil
    2 tablespoons snipped fresh oregano
    2 tablespoons snipped fresh chives
    1 teaspoon kosher salt or ½ teaspoon
       table salt
    1 teaspoon cracked black pepper
    1 teaspoon olive oil (optional)
    1 8-ounce loaf baguette-style French bread,
       cut into ¼-inch-thick slices
       Assorted vegetable dippers

1. In a large mixing bowl, beat ricotta on medium speed for 2 minutes. Add Parmesan. Beat until combined. Stir in basil, oregano, chives, salt and pepper. (If the spread seems dry, stir in olive oil.)

2. Spoon spread into a serving bowl. Chill, covered, for 1 hour or up to 12 hours.

3. Place bread slices on a large baking sheet. Bake in a 425° oven about 5 minutes or until lightly toasted. Turn slices over. Bake about 3 minutes more or until second sides are lightly toasted.

4. Serve spread with cooled toast slices and vegetable dippers. **Makes 16 servings.**

Per 2 tablespoons: 120 cal, 5 g fat, 17 mg chol, 347 mg sodium, 12 g carbo, 1 g fiber, 7 g pro.

Candles create a sense of enchantment at Avon Gardens outside Indianapolis. Avon Gardens has been described as part nursery, part botanical garden and part muse.

RICOTTA AND
PARMESAN SPREAD

MINI PARTY
QUICHES

Mini Party Quiches

These two-bite appetizers have a crisp Parmesan crust and a savory custard filling.

PREP 30 minutes **BAKE** 28 minutes **COOL** 5 minutes

Nonstick cooking spray
2 cups all-purpose flour
2 tablespoons grated Parmesan cheese
½ teaspoon salt
⅓ cup olive oil or vegetable oil (such as canola)
5 to 7 tablespoons ice-cold water
1 egg
⅓ cup milk
Dash ground black pepper
⅓ cup finely shredded Monterey Jack or Gruyère cheese
1 tablespoon chopped green onion
5 or 6 pear or cherry tomatoes, thinly sliced (optional)
24 small herb leaves (optional)

1. Coat twenty-four 1¾-inch muffin cups with cooking spray; set aside. For pastry: In a large bowl stir together flour, Parmesan cheese and salt. Add oil all at once. Mix until crumbly. Add 2 tablespoons of the ice-cold water; stir to combine. Add enough remaining water, 1 tablespoon at a time, until flour is moistened. Gather into a ball, then knead gently just until pastry holds together.

2. Divide pastry into 24 portions. Press each portion into a prepared muffin cup. Do not prick. Bake in a 425° oven for 8 to 10 minutes or just until pastry begins to brown. Remove from oven; set aside. Reduce oven to 350°.

3. For quiche filling: In a small bowl, whisk together egg, milk and pepper. Stir in Monterey Jack cheese and onion. Fill each pastry cup with about 1 teaspoon filling. If you like, top each quiche with a tomato slice and/or herb leaves.

4. Bake quiches in 350° oven about 20 minutes or until filling is puffed and set. Cool in muffin cups on a wire rack for 5 minutes. Remove from cups; serve warm. **Makes 24 quiches.**

Per 2 quiches: 156 cal, 8 g fat, 20 mg chol, 141 mg sodium, 17 g carbo, 1 g fiber, 4 g pro.

Cheese and Almond Guacamole

Serrano peppers are slightly smaller and hotter than jalapeños. If you like guacamole spicy, add the peppers seeds and all, or remove the seeds to reduce the heat.

START TO FINISH 20 minutes

4 avocados, halved, seeded, peeled and coarsely chopped
½ cup chopped red onion
2 serrano peppers,* halved, seeded and finely chopped
¾ cup crumbled feta or goat cheese (6 ounces)
1 lime, juiced
½ cup sliced almonds, toasted and chopped
⅓ cup chopped fresh cilantro
¾ teaspoon salt
Carrots, jicama strips and/or pita chips
Lime wedges and cilantro sprigs (optional)

1. In a large bowl, combine the avocados, onion and serrano peppers; mash slightly with a fork. Fold in the cheese, lime juice, almonds, chopped cilantro and salt. Spoon into serving bowl. Serve at once or cover surface directly with plastic wrap and refrigerate for up to 6 hours.

2. Serve with carrots, jicama strips and/or pita chips and, if you like, lime wedges and cilantro sprigs. **Makes about 10 (¼-cup) servings.**

*Tip: Because hot chile peppers contain oils that can burn your skin and eyes, avoid direct contact with them as much as possible. When working with chile peppers, wear plastic or rubber gloves. If bare hands do touch the chile peppers, wash your hands well with soap and water.

Per ¼ cup: 183 cal, 16 g fat, 13 mg chol, 268 mg sodium, 8 g carbo, 5 g fiber, 6 g pro.

Double-Strawberry Scones

These flaky scones include both fresh and freeze-dried strawberries. Basil adds a touch of bright, snappy flavor that complements the berries.

PREP 25 minutes **BAKE** 16 minutes

2½ cups all-purpose flour
  2 tablespoons sugar
  1 tablespoon baking powder
  ¼ teaspoon salt
  ½ cup cold butter, cut into chunks
  ¾ cup chopped fresh strawberries
  ½ cup freeze-dried strawberries
  2 tablespoons snipped fresh basil
  2 eggs, lightly beaten
  ½ cup half-and-half
    Half-and-half or milk
    Sugar

1. In a large bowl, stir together flour, the 2 tablespoons sugar, baking powder and salt. Using a pastry blender or two knives, cut in butter until mixture resembles coarse crumbs. Gently toss in fresh and freeze-dried strawberries and basil. Make a well in center of flour mixture; set aside.

2. In a medium bowl, stir together eggs and the ½ cup half-and-half. Add egg mixture to flour mixture all at once. Using a large spoon, gently stir just until moistened.

3. Turn dough out onto a generously floured surface. Knead dough by folding and gently pressing it five to seven times, turning dough a quarter turn after each fold. Transfer to a baking sheet lined with parchment paper and lightly sprinkled with flour. Pat or lightly roll dough into a ¾-inch-thick circle. Cut circle into wedges and pull apart slightly.

4. Brush wedges with additional half-and-half and sprinkle with sugar. Bake in a 400° oven about 16 minutes or until golden. Serve warm. Refrigerate leftover scones; reheat 15 seconds in microwave. **Makes 12 scones.**

Per scone: 209 cal, 10 g fat, 60 mg chol, 211 mg sodium, 26 g carbo, 1 g fiber, 4 g pro.

The fresh flavors of spring are a welcome change after the hearty, heavy foods of winter. Celebrate a sunny morning with strawberry-studded scones—and a warm evening with a spring greens-topped grilled pizza.

Grilled Onion Flatbread with Bacon and Arugula

Begin the outdoor cooking season with an appetizer straight off the grill.

PREP 10 minutes **GRILL** 8 minutes

  4 small red onions
  1 tablespoon olive oil
    Salt
    Freshly ground black pepper
  6 ounces cream cheese, softened
  ¼ cup strong dark ale, such as Chimay
    (a Belgian beer)
  2 teaspoons Worcestershire sauce
    Pinch cayenne pepper
  2 10-inch packaged soft flatbreads
1½ cups torn arugula
  1 cup cherry tomatoes, halved or quartered
  6 slices crisp-cooked bacon, crumbled

1. Peel and halve onions. Brush with oil, then sprinkle with salt and black pepper.

2. Grill onions on the rack of a covered charcoal or gas grill directly over medium-high heat for 6 to 8 minutes or until charred and slightly softened, turning once halfway through grilling. Cool.

3. In a medium bowl, whisk together cream cheese, ale, Worcestershire sauce and cayenne pepper until smooth. Chop two grilled onions; stir into cream cheese mixture. Season to taste with additional salt and black pepper. Quarter remaining two onions; set aside.

4. Grill flatbreads on rack of a covered grill directly over medium-high heat for 2 to 4 minutes or until crisp, turning once halfway through. Transfer to cutting board. Spread half of cream cheese mixture onto each flatbread. Top with arugula, tomatoes, bacon and quartered onions. Slice and serve. **Makes 8 servings.**

Per serving: 230 cal, 13 g fat, 32 mg chol, 589 mg sodium, 20 g carbo, 1 g fiber, 7 g pro.

GRILLED ONION FLATBREAD WITH BACON AND ARUGULA

HEARTY WAFFLES

Hearty Waffles

PREP 15 minutes **COOK** 4 minutes per batch

    Nonstick cooking spray
1 pint strawberries, hulled and sliced
1 tablespoon granulated sugar
1½ cups all-purpose flour
1¼ cups white whole wheat flour
½ cup packed brown sugar
¼ cup wheat germ
2 teaspoons baking powder
½ teaspoon pumpkin pie spice
¾ teaspoon baking soda
½ teaspoon salt
1¾ cups low-fat buttermilk
¾ cup water
2 eggs, separated
2 tablespoons canola oil
1 teaspoon vanilla extract
1 tablespoon powdered sugar

1. Preheat oven to 200°. Heat a Belgian waffle maker per manufacturer's directions. Lightly coat with nonstick cooking spray.

2. For topping: Combine berries and granulated sugar in a bowl. Set aside.

3. For waffles: In a bowl, combine flours, brown sugar, wheat germ, baking powder, pumpkin pie spice, baking soda and salt.

4. In a bowl, combine buttermilk, the water, egg yolks, oil and vanilla. In a small mixing bowl, beat egg whites to stiff peaks.

5. Mix buttermilk mixture into flour mixture. Fold in egg whites. Pour ½ cup batter onto each section of prepared waffle maker. Cook per manufacturer's instructions, about 4 minutes per batch. Transfer waffles directly to oven rack in 200° oven. Repeat. Serve waffles with topping and sprinkle with powdered sugar.
Makes twelve 4-inch waffles.

Per 2 waffles + ⅓ cup topping: 377 cal, 8 g fat, 75 mg chol, 594 mg sodium; 65 g carbo, 6 g fiber, 13 g pro.

Apricot-Raisin Hot Cross Buns

PREP 35 minutes **RISE** 2 hours 15 minutes **BAKE** 12 minutes

4 to 4½ cups all-purpose flour
1 package active dry yeast
¼ cup warm water (110°)
⅛ teaspoon sugar
¾ cup milk
½ cup butter
⅓ cup sugar
½ teaspoon salt
2 eggs
½ cup finely snipped dried apricots
½ cup raisins, coarsely chopped
1 egg white, beaten
1 tablespoon water
    Dried apricots, cut into strips (optional)

1. In a large mixing bowl, place 2 cups of the flour; set aside. In a bowl, combine the yeast, the warm water and ⅛ teaspoon sugar. Stir until yeast is dissolved; set aside. In a medium saucepan, heat and stir the milk, butter, ⅓ cup sugar and salt until warm (120° to 130°) and butter is almost melted. Add to flour along with yeast mixture and eggs. Beat with an electric mixer on low speed for 30 seconds, scraping sides of bowl constantly. Beat on high speed for 3 minutes. Stir in snipped apricots, raisins and as much of the remaining flour as you can with a wooden spoon.

2. Turn dough out onto a lightly floured surface. Knead in enough remaining flour to make a moderately soft (not sticky) dough that is smooth and elastic (3 to 5 minutes total). Shape dough into a ball. Place dough in a lightly greased bowl, turning once to grease surface of dough. Let rise, covered, in a warm place until double in size (about 1½ hours).

3. Punch down dough. Turn out onto a floured surface. Let rest, covered, for 10 minutes. Divide dough into 20 portions; shape each into a smooth ball. Place balls 2 inches apart on two greased baking sheets. Let rise, covered, until nearly double (45 to 60 minutes).

4. Make a crisscross slash across top of each bun with a sharp knife or scissors. In a small cup, combine beaten egg white and the water; brush on buns. Bake for 12 to 15 minutes or until golden brown, rotating baking sheets halfway through baking. If you like, top with apricot strips. Serve warm. Store remaining buns in an airtight container in the refrigerator up to 3 days. To reheat, place one or two buns at a time on a microwave-safe plate and heat on low (30% power) for 15 to 20 seconds.
Makes 20 buns.

Per bun: 177 cal, 6 g fat, 34 mg chol, 106 mg sodium, 28 g carbo, 1 g fiber, 4 g pro.

Symbolizing life's journey, a single path leads to the center of the free-admission Harmonist Labyrinth in The Roofless Church outside of New Harmony, Indiana. Founded as a Utopian community in 1814, the hamlet of nearly 900 souls is now something of an artists' colony, with galleries, restaurants, art festivals and a concert series.

GRILLED STEAK WITH
CHIMICHURRI AND
MOLE BBQ SAUCES

Grilled Steak

Slice just before serving, then let guests choose between vinegary herb-packed Chimichurri Sauce and velvety cocoa-laced Mole BBQ Sauce. Make both sauces ahead of time so you'll be back mingling with the crowd, drink in hand, in no time.

PREP 15 minutes **STAND** 25 minutes
GRILL 16 minutes

   3 pounds beef flank steak
   2 teaspoons kosher salt
   2 teaspoons smoked paprika
   1 teaspoon packed brown sugar
   ½ teaspoon ground ancho chile pepper
   ½ teaspoon ground black pepper
      Chimichurri Sauce (see recipe, right)
        (optional)
      Mole BBQ Sauce (see recipe, right)
        (optional)

1. Rinse steak; pat steak dry with paper towels. For rub, in a small bowl, combine salt, smoked paprika, brown sugar, ancho chile pepper and black pepper. Sprinkle rub over steak; pat evenly onto meat. Let steak stand for 20 minutes at room temperature before grilling.

2. Heat a charcoal or gas grill to medium. Scrape grill clean; coat with oil. Grill steak, covered, for 8 to 10 minutes per side until medium rare (145°).

3. Remove steaks from grill; let stand for 5 minutes. Slice crosswise into ⅛-inch slices. If you like, serve with Chimichurri Sauce or Mole BBQ Sauce. **Makes 8 servings.**

Make-ahead directions: Cover and chill seasoned, uncooked steak up to 8 hours before grilling.

Per serving: 386 cal, 23 g fat, 111 mg chol, 741 mg sodium, 6 g carbo, 2 g fiber, 37 g pro.

Chimichurri Sauce

Stirring in the vinegar right before serving keeps this sauce a brilliant green.

START TO FINISH 10 minutes

   2 cups packed fresh parsley leaves and
        small stems
   1 cup packed fresh cilantro leaves and
        small stems
   ½ cup extra virgin olive oil
   ⅓ cup coarsely chopped red sweet pepper
   ¼ cup water
   2 tablespoons coarsely chopped onion
   3 cloves garlic, coarsely chopped
   ¾ teaspoon kosher salt
   ½ teaspoon dried oregano, crushed
   ⅛ to ¼ teaspoon crushed red pepper
   ⅛ teaspoon ground black pepper
   ⅛ teaspoon sugar
   2½ tablespoons sherry vinegar

In a blender container or food processor, combine parsley, cilantro, oil, sweet pepper, water, onion, garlic, salt, oregano, crushed red pepper, black pepper and sugar. Cover; blend or process until finely chopped, stopping to scrape down sides. Transfer to bowl; stir in vinegar before serving. **Makes 10 servings.**

Make-ahead directions: Prepare sauce without vinegar. Chill in an airtight container up to 2 days or freeze for longer storage. Bring to room temperature; stir in vinegar just before serving.

Per serving: 104 cal, 11 g fat, 0 g chol, 156 mg sodium, 2 g carbo, 1 g fiber, 1 g pro.

Mole BBQ Sauce

The undercurrent of cocoa gives this sauce its deep earthy flavor. Try it on anything from pork to chicken.

PREP 10 minutes **COOK** 2 minutes

   ¾ cup ketchup
   2 tablespoons butter, chopped
   1 tablespoon packed dark brown sugar
   1 tablespoon unsweetened cocoa powder
        (not Dutch-process)
   1 tablespoon water
   1 tablespoon cider vinegar
   1 tablespoon molasses
   1½ teaspoons yellow mustard
   1½ teaspoons Worcestershire sauce
   ¾ teaspoon smoked paprika
   ¾ teaspoon ground ancho chile pepper
   ½ teaspoon kosher salt
   ½ teaspoon dried oregano, crushed
   ¼ teaspoon garlic powder
   ¼ teaspoon onion powder
   ¼ teaspoon ground cinnamon
   ⅛ teaspoon ground black pepper

In a small heatproof bowl, combine all ingredients. Microwave on 100 percent power (high) for 2 to 3 minutes or until hot and bubbly, stopping once to stir. Cool and serve. **Makes 8 servings.**

Make-ahead directions: Chill sauce up to 1 week. Bring sauce to room temperature before serving.

Per serving: 71 cal, 3 g fat, 8 mg chol, 375 mg sodium, 10 g carbo, 0 g fiber, 1 g pro.

Steak Sandwiches

If you'd like to use a Wisconsin blue cheese, chefs at The Iron Horse Hotel in Milwaukee recommend Salemville Blue Cheese Crumbles or Carr Valley's Billy Blue, but any supermarket blue will work.

PREP 20 minutes **COOK** 33 minutes **GRILL** 5 minutes

2 tablespoons butter
4 cups thinly sliced onion (4 large)
1 tablespoon snipped fresh thyme or
    1 teaspoon dried thyme, crushed
1 teaspoon sugar
1 teaspoon salt
½ teaspoon freshly ground black pepper
1 pound beef tenderloin
⅛ teaspoon ground black pepper
4 ounces crumbled blue cheese
4 teaspoons butter
4 sourdough buns or kaiser rolls, split

1. For caramelized onions: In a large nonstick skillet, melt butter over medium-low heat. Add onion. Cook, covered, for 15 minutes, stirring occasionally. Uncover; stir in thyme, sugar, salt and the ½ teaspoon pepper. Cook, stirring occasionally, over medium-high heat for 14 to 16 minutes more or until onion is tender and golden. Set aside.

2. Trim fat from meat. Cut meat crosswise into four slices. Place each meat slice between two pieces of plastic wrap. Use the flat side of a meat mallet or a rolling pin to lightly pound meat to ½-inch thickness. Discard plastic wrap. Season beef with ⅛ teaspoon pepper.

3. For a charcoal grill, place meat on rack of uncovered grill directly over medium coals. Grill steak for 3 minutes, turning once halfway through. (For a gas grill: Preheat grill. Reduce heat to medium. Place meat on grill rack over heat. Cover; grill as directed.) Remove meat from grill. Top each steak with a quarter of the caramelized onions and blue cheese. Return meat to grill. Grill for 2 to 3 minutes more or until cheese begins to melt.

4. Meanwhile, heat 2 teaspoons butter on a griddle over medium heat. Lay two buns, cut sides down, on griddle pan. Toast for 2 to 3 minutes or until golden. Repeat with remaining butter and buns. Serve steaks on toasted buns. **Makes 4 sandwiches.**

Per sandwich: 696 cal, 43 g fat, 122 mg chol, 1,421 mg sodium, 43 g carbo, 3 g fiber, 33 g pro.

Midwesterners celebrate spring in many ways. We hunt for morels, cut confetti-color bouquets, savor radishes and rhubarb—and, of course, spread the beauty of spring flowers around our yards. Daffodils, which grow in profusion in Midwest gardens, are a perennial favorite.

Crispy Honey-Mustard Pork Chops

A quick chill in the fridge lets the marinade thicken and adhere to the pork chops. Serve the chops with Sweet Beet Chutney.

PREP 15 minutes **MARINATE** 5 minutes **COOK** 6 minutes **BAKE** 8 minutes

4 pork chops, ½ inch thick (about
    1½ pounds)
½ teaspoon salt
¼ teaspoon freshly ground black pepper
¼ cup honey
¼ cup stone-ground mustard
2 tablespoons panko bread crumbs
2 teaspoons chopped fresh marjoram
⅛ teaspoon onion powder
¼ cup extra virgin olive oil
    Sweet Beet Chutney (recipe follows)

1. Trim fat from pork chops, season with salt and pepper, then set aside. In a shallow dish, combine honey and mustard. In a small bowl, combine bread crumbs, 1 teaspoon of the marjoram and the onion powder. Set aside.

2. Dip chops in honey mixture to coat, letting excess drip off. Place on a plate lined with parchment paper. Marinate in refrigerator 5 minutes.

3. Heat a very large skillet over medium-high heat. Swirl in olive oil. (If pan isn't large enough to hold 4 chops without crowding, cook in two batches.) Cook chops in hot oil about 3 minutes or until undersides are crisp and browned. Turn chops; cook for 3 minutes. Transfer to oven-safe platter. Sprinkle chops with bread crumb mixture.

4. Bake chops in a 450° oven for 8 to 9 minutes or until crumbs begin to brown. Sprinkle with remaining marjoram. Serve with Sweet Beet Chutney. **Makes 4 servings.**

Per serving: 553 cal, 25 g fat, 64 mg chol, 783 mg sodium, 58 g carbo, 4 g fiber, 26 g pro.

Sweet Beet Chutney: In a medium saucepan, combine 1 pound peeled and diced beets and ¾ cup water. Cover saucepan and bring to boiling; reduce heat. Boil gently, covered, for 8 minutes. Uncover. Stir in ½ cup raisins, ¼ cup cider vinegar, 3 tablespoons honey, 1 teaspoon ground coriander, ½ teaspoon dried mustard, ½ teaspoon ground cardamom and salt to taste. Return to gentle boiling. Cook, uncovered, for 20 to 25 minutes or until liquid is syrupy and beets are tender.

Honey acts as a foil for zingy ingredients like mustard. But don't be fooled into thinking it's all about sweet. A squeeze of honey glazes earthy beets and exotic spices unleash distinctive, heady notes.

Greens, Egg and Ham Loaf

If prepared ahead, reheat by the slice in a microwave or a skillet. Because of the ground ham, this loaf will be a little pink even when fully cooked because of the ground ham.

PREP 30 minutes **BAKE** 1 hour **STAND** 10 minutes

2 eggs
⅓ cup apple cider
⅔ cup quick-cooking rolled oats
⅓ cup chopped green onion (3)
1 tablespoon Dijon-style mustard
½ teaspoon poultry seasoning
¼ teaspoon ground black pepper
12 ounces ground pork
12 ounces ground cooked ham
2 tablespoons vegetable oil
8 eggs
Salt and black pepper
2 6-ounce packages fresh baby spinach
Quick Dill Sauce (recipe follows)
Fresh dill (optional)

1. In a large bowl, beat two eggs and cider with a wire whisk to combine. Stir in oats, green onion, mustard, poultry seasoning and pepper. Add pork and ham; mix well. Lightly pat mixture into an 8x4x2-inch loaf pan.

2. Bake in a 350° oven for 1 to 1¼ hours or until an instant-read thermometer inserted into center of loaf registers 160°. Spoon off fat. Let stand for 10 minutes before serving.

3. Meanwhile, in a large skillet, heat 1 tablespoon oil over medium heat. Break four eggs into skillet. Sprinkle with salt and pepper. Reduce heat to low. Cook, covered, for 3 to 4 minutes or until whites are completely set and yolks start to thicken. Repeat with remaining eggs. Remove from skillet; cover and keep warm.

4. Wipe out skillet with paper towel, if needed. In the skillet, cook spinach, half at a time, in the remaining 1 tablespoon oil just until wilted. Remove from pan.

5. To serve, divide spinach between eight plates. Top with ham loaf slice, egg, Quick Dill Sauce and, if you like, fresh dill.
Makes 8 servings.

Quick Dill Sauce: In a small saucepan, stir together ½ cup sour cream, ½ cup mayonnaise, 2 teaspoons cider vinegar and 1 teaspoon Dijon mustard. Cook and stir over low heat until hot. Stir in 1 teaspoon snipped fresh dill. Thin with milk if needed.

Per serving: 369 cal, 29 g fat, 125 mg chol, 736 mg sodium, 9 g carbo, 2 g fiber, 19 g pro.

A landscape that has spent months in neutral now bursts with color. A sweep of soft-petaled tulips is the perfect place for an Easter egg hunt.

MEAT AND
POTATO PIZZA

Meat and Potato Pizza

This potato-topped pizza is not for the carb-adverse—but it sure is good!

PREP 20 minutes **BAKE** 14 minutes **STAND** 2 minutes

3 tablespoons butter, softened
4 cloves garlic, minced
1 teaspoon snipped fresh rosemary
1 13.8-ounce package refrigerated pizza dough
2 russet potatoes (about 10 ounces), peeled and very thinly sliced
7 ounces cooked smoked sausage, thinly sliced
5 slices bacon, crisp-cooked and crumbled
1 cup shredded mozzarella cheese (4 ounces)

1. In a small bowl, combine butter, garlic and rosemary.

2. Unroll pizza dough into a 15x10x1-inch baking pan. Press out to a 14x10-inch rectangle. Pinch edges to form a rim. Spread butter mixture over dough. Top with potatoes, sausage, bacon and cheese.

3. Bake in a 425° oven for 14 to 16 minutes or until crust is golden brown and potatoes are tender. (There may be butter in the pan.) Let stand at least 2 minutes before slicing. **Makes 4 servings.**

Per serving: 669 cal, 36 g fat, 78 mg chol, 1,661 mg sodium, 62 g carbo, 3 g fiber, 26 g pro.

Italian Dinner Soup

On a cool spring night, this quick-to-fix soup is warming and comforting.

START TO FINISH 30 minutes

1 pound uncooked Italian sausage links, casings removed (about 4)
3 cups chicken stock or broth
3 cups beef stock or broth
1 14.5-ounce can diced tomatoes with basil, garlic and oregano, undrained
1 9-ounce package refrigerated ravioli
2 cups baby spinach leaves, chopped
¼ cup fresh basil leaves, chopped
2 ounces Parmesan cheese, grated

1. In a large skillet, cook sausage over medium-low heat until no pink remains, stirring to break up. Drain and set aside.

2. Meanwhile, in a Dutch oven, combine chicken stock, beef stock and undrained tomatoes; bring to boiling. Add ravioli and cook 7 minutes. Add sausage; return to boiling. Stir in spinach to wilt, then add basil. Top each serving with cheese. **Makes 6 servings.**

Per 1¾ cups: 486 cal, 30 g fat, 89 mg chol, 1,784 mg sodium, 27 g carbo, 2 g fiber, 26 g pro.

Long before sweet and salty became a fad, Great Plains Sauce and Dough Company in Ames, Iowa, offered honey with its pizza for drizzling over the last bites of its famous Denver-style crust—a yeasty whole wheat handful of chewy goodness.

Herbed Chicken with Spring Vegetables

A springy mix of herbs, garlic and lemon works magic when cooked inside this roasted chicken.

PREP 1 hours **GRILL** 1 hour 10 minutes **STAND** 10 minutes

¼ cup snipped fresh Italian (flat-leaf) parsley
2 tablespoons snipped fresh tarragon
2 teaspoons lemon zest
½ teaspoon salt
1 4½- to 5-pound whole roasting chicken
1 lemon wedge or ½ of a Meyer lemon
4 cloves garlic, halved and smashed
3 sprigs fresh Italian (flat-leaf) parsley
2 sprigs fresh tarragon
1 tablespoon olive oil
1½ pounds assorted small new potatoes, halved or quartered
2 cloves garlic, minced
2 tablespoons olive oil
1 pound asparagus, trimmed and cut into 3-inch pieces
6 thick green onions, tops trimmed
2 small Meyer lemons, halved (optional)
Sea salt

1. In a small bowl, combine the ¼ cup parsley, the 2 tablespoons tarragon, lemon zest and salt. Reserve 2 tablespoons of the herb mixture for the vegetables. Cover and set aside.

2. Rinse chicken cavity; pat dry with paper towels. Using your fingers, loosen the skin on the chicken breast and legs. Carefully spoon 2 tablespoons of the remaining herb mixture under the skin of the chicken.

3. Add lemon wedge, four smashed garlic cloves, three sprigs of parsley and two sprigs tarragon to the cavity of the chicken. Brush the surface of chicken skin with 1 tablespoon olive oil. Pat remaining herbs onto the surface of the chicken; set aside. Place the chicken on a rack in a roasting pan.

4. For a charcoal grill: arrange medium-hot coals around a drip pan. Test for medium heat above pan. Place the roasting pan in the center of the grill; cover and grill for 50 minutes.

5. Meanwhile, place potatoes in a large microwave-safe bowl. Add the 2 cloves minced garlic and 1 tablespoon of the olive oil; stir to coat. Cover bowl with waxed paper. Microwave on 100 percent power (high) for 8 minutes, stirring twice. Add asparagus, green onions and, if you like, lemon halves. Drizzle with remaining 1 tablespoon olive oil. Sprinkle with sea salt. Toss to evenly coat vegetables.

6. Add prepared vegetables to the roasting pan; cover and grill for 20 to 25 minutes more or until chicken is no longer pink (170° in thigh muscle). Remove pan from the grill. Sprinkle the reserved 2 tablespoons of herb mixture over vegetables. Cover pan with foil; let stand 10 minutes. (The temperature of the chicken will rise to 180° while standing.)

7. Serve chicken with vegetables.
Makes 6 servings.

Per serving: 479 cal, 25 g fat, 116 mg chol, 425 mg sodium, 24 g carbo, 4 g fiber, 40 g pro.

Spinach-Mushroom-Sausage Pierogi Bake

This quick casserole taps our region's ethnic roots. Pierogies are half-moon-shape dumplings of Polish origin.

PREP 25 minutes **BAKE** 30 minutes

- 1 16-ounce package frozen potato pierogies
- 1 small onion, chopped
- 1 tablespoon olive oil
- 4 cooked chicken sausages, sliced (12 ounces)
- 1 8-ounce package sliced mushrooms
- 1 clove garlic, minced
- 1 10-ounce package frozen chopped spinach, thawed and squeezed dry
- 1 3-ounce package cream cheese, cut up
- ¼ cup chicken broth
- ½ teaspoon salt
- ¼ teaspoon ground black pepper
- ½ cup shredded mozzarella cheese

1. Place the frozen pierogies in a 2-quart rectangular baking dish; set aside. In a large saucepan, cook onion in hot oil for 2 to 3 minutes or just until tender. Stir in sliced sausage, mushrooms and garlic. Cook and stir for 3 minutes more. Add the spinach, cream cheese, chicken broth, salt and pepper. Cook and stir over medium heat to melt cream cheese. Pour the sausage mixture over the pierogies. Sprinkle with mozzarella cheese.

2. Bake, uncovered, in a 400° oven about 30 minutes or until lightly browned and heated through. **Makes 6 servings.**

Per serving: 339 cal, 18 g fat, 81 mg chol, 1,204 mg sodium, 29 g carbo, 2 g fiber, 18 g pro.

The White Burger

Wondering about a white burger? This one is made with ground turkey breast and topped with white cheddar and wine-poached pears.

PREP 20 minutes **COOK** 13 minutes

- 1 ripe Bartlett pear, thinly sliced
- ½ cup dry white wine
- 1½ tablespoons lemon juice
- 1 pound ground uncooked turkey breast
- 2 green onions, finely chopped
- ½ to 1 tablespoon Dijon-style mustard
- 1 teaspoon lemon zest
- 1½ teaspoons snipped fresh thyme
- ½ teaspoon salt
- ¼ teaspoon ground black pepper
- 1 tablespoon olive oil
- 1 cup shredded sharp white cheddar cheese (4 ounces)
- 4 tablespoons jalapeño jelly
- 4 ciabatta rolls, split and toasted

1. In a medium skillet, combine the pear slices, wine, lemon juice and enough water to just cover the pear. Bring to boiling. Reduce heat; simmer about 5 minutes or until the pear softens. Using a slotted spoon, remove pear and set aside.

2. Meanwhile, in a large bowl, combine the turkey, green onions, mustard, lemon zest, thyme, salt and pepper. Shape turkey mixture into four patties.

3. In a large nonstick skillet, cook patties in hot olive oil over medium heat for 8 to 10 minutes or until no longer pink (170°), turning once. Top with pears and cheese. Cover and cook until cheese melts, about 2 minutes. Spread 1 tablespoon jelly on each roll bottom. Top with a burger and roll top. **Makes 4 servings.**

Per serving: 465 cal, 14 g fat, 85 mg chol, 964 mg sodium, 42 g carbo, 6 g fiber, 36 g pro.

THE WHITE BURGER

**WALLEYE WILD RICE
CAKES WITH WASABI
DRESSING**

Walleye Wild Rice Cakes with Wasabi Dressing

These fish and rice cakes call on two Minnesota staples. The wasabi dressing provides a zippy, Asian addition.

PREP 30 minutes **CHILL** 2 hours **COOK** 10 minutes

- 8 ounces skinned walleye, sole or tilapia fillets, thawed, if frozen
- ½ cup dry white wine
- 1 egg, lightly beaten
- 1 cup panko bread crumbs
- ½ cup cooked wild rice
- ¼ cup finely chopped onion
- 2 tablespoons finely chopped red sweet pepper
- 2 tablespoons canola oil mayonnaise or regular mayonnaise
- 1 tablespoon Dijon-style mustard
- 1 tablespoon Worcestershire sauce
- 1 teaspoon lemon juice
- ¼ teaspoon salt
- ¼ teaspoon ground black pepper
- 2 tablespoons canola oil
- Wasabi Dressing (recipe follows)
- Mixed greens (optional)

1. Rinse fish; pat dry with paper towels. Pour wine over fish in a 2-quart baking dish. Bake in a 450° oven, uncovered, for 4 to 6 minutes per ½-inch thickness of fish or until fish flakes when tested with a fork. Drain and break into pieces.

2. In a medium bowl, combine fish, egg, panko, wild rice, onion, red sweet pepper, mayonnaise, mustard, Worcestershire sauce, lemon juice, salt and pepper. Shape into six ¾-inch patties. Place on a baking sheet; cover and chill for 2 hours.

3. In a very large skillet, cook patties in hot canola oil over medium heat for 10 minutes or until golden brown, turning once. Serve with Wasabi Dressing and, if you like, mixed greens. **Makes 3 servings.**

Wasabi Dressing: In a small bowl, combine ¼ cup canola oil mayonnaise or regular mayonnaise, ½ teaspoon lemon juice, ½ teaspoon prepared wasabi paste, ½ teaspoon sugar and ¼ teaspoon soy sauce. Season with salt and ground black pepper.

Per serving: 415 cal, 21 g fat, 127 mg chol, 817 mg sodium, 25 g carbo, 1 g fiber, 20 g pro.

Asparagus-Tuna Casserole

PREP 20 minutes **COOK** 20 minutes
BAKE 25 minutes

- 1 cup dried penne pasta
- 1 pound tiny new potatoes, cut into ½-inch dice
- 3 tablespoons butter
- ¼ cup chopped onion
- 2 tablespoons all-purpose flour
- 2¼ cups milk
- 2 teaspoons lemon zest
- 4 ounces provolone cheese, shredded
- 1½ pounds green, white and/or purple asparagus, trimmed and cut into 1-inch pieces
- 3 4.5-ounce cans tuna packed in roasted garlic olive oil or desired flavor tuna
- ½ cup pitted kalamata olives, halved
- ¼ cup soft bread crumbs
- ¼ cup finely shredded Parmesan cheese

1. In a large saucepan, cook pasta according to package directions, adding potatoes during the last 4 minutes of cooking time. Drain and set aside.

2. Meanwhile, for sauce: In a large Dutch oven, melt 2 tablespoons of the butter. Cook onion in butter about 3 minutes or until tender. Stir in flour and a pinch each salt and ground black pepper. Cook and stir 2 minutes more. Whisk in milk all at once. Add lemon zest. Cook and stir until thickened and bubbly. Whisk in provolone cheese until melted. Gently fold pasta, potatoes, asparagus, tuna and olives into sauce. Pour into a 3-quart rectangular baking dish.

3. For topping: In a small bowl, melt the remaining 1 tablespoon of butter. Stir in bread crumbs and Parmesan. Sprinkle on casserole. Bake, uncovered, in a 375° oven for 25 to 30 minutes, until heated through and topping is golden. **Makes 6 servings.**

Per serving: 467 cal, 21 g fat, 50 mg chol, 753 mg sodium, 36 g carbo, 5 g fiber, 34 g pro.

Roasted Asparagus-Orange Salad

For an even simpler roasted asparagus side dish, prepare through Step 1 and serve.

PREP 10 minutes **ROAST** 15 minutes

    2 pounds green, white and/or purple
        asparagus, trimmed
    1 tablespoon olive oil
    ¼ teaspoon salt
    2 oranges
    2 tablespoons olive oil
    1 tablespoon cider vinegar
    1 clove garlic, minced
    1 teaspoon Dijon-style mustard
    ½ teaspoon fennel seeds, crushed

1. Place asparagus in a 15x10x1-inch baking pan. Drizzle with 1 tablespoon oil and sprinkle with salt; toss to coat. Roast, uncovered, in a 400° oven for 15 to 20 minutes or until asparagus is crisp-tender, tossing once. Transfer asparagus to a serving platter.

2. Meanwhile, for dressing: Zest one orange for 1 teaspoon; set aside. Juice half an orange. Peel and slice the remaining oranges into rounds. In a jar with tight-fitting lid, combine orange zest, orange juice, 2 tablespoons olive oil, the vinegar, garlic, mustard and fennel seeds. Cover and shake to combine.

3. Drizzle a little of the dressing on the asparagus; toss to coat. Carefully toss in orange slices. Pass remaining dressing. **Makes 8 servings.**

Per serving: 85 cal, 5 g fat, 0 mg chol, 90 mg sodium, 8 g carbo, 3 g fiber, 3 g pro.

Garden Veggie Linguine with Cilantro Pesto

The outdoors beckons. Whip up this fresh and fast supper, then go for a stroll to smell the lilacs.

START TO FINISH 30 minutes

    8 ounces dry linguine or fettuccine
    8 ounces baby zucchini, halved lengthwise,
        or 1 small zucchini, sliced
    8 ounce package peeled fresh baby carrots,
        halved
    2 seedless oranges
    1 cup fresh cilantro leaves
    ½ cup olive oil
    1 teaspoon salt
    1 teaspoon dry mustard
    1 teaspoon minced garlic or dried garlic
    ½ teaspoon crushed red pepper
        Cilantro and/or orange zest (optional)

1. Cook pasta according to package directions, adding zucchini and carrots the last 5 minutes. Drain; reserve ¼ cup pasta water. Return pasta to pan.

2. For pesto: Peel and quarter one orange. In a food processor, combine the quartered orange, reserved pasta water, cilantro, olive oil, salt, mustard, garlic and crushed red pepper. Cover and process until almost smooth.

3. Peel and chop the remaining orange. Add pesto and orange to pasta in pan. Toss to combine. If you like, top with cilantro and/or orange zest. **Makes 4 servings.**

Per serving: 518 cal, 28 g fat, 0 mg chol, 644 mg sodium, 58 g carbo, 6 g fiber, 10 g pro.

When making Garden Veggie Linguine with Cilantro Pesto, try substituting a variety of fresh in-season vegetables and herbs—asparagus, snap peas, spinach or mustard greens, tarragon, basil or other colorful veggies and herbs that catch your eye at the farmers' market.

GARDEN VEGGIE
LINGUINE WITH
CILANTRO PESTO

On a private wooded slope in Elkhart, Illinois, Mother Nature sweeps away winter in a glorious wash of blue and green. Virginia bluebells and other wildflowers carpet Elkhart Hill, a rare high point on the glacier-flattened landscape between St. Louis and Chicago.

STRAWBERRY AND
ARUGULA SALAD WITH
MANCHEGO FRICOS

Strawberry and Arugula Salad with Manchego Fricos

Italian for "little trifles," fricos are lacy wafers of crispy fried cheese. They're made by cooking small piles of finely shredded cheese in a skillet until the cheese starts to bubble and brown around the edges. Sometimes a bit of flour or herbs is mixed in. They are absolutely delicious on salads or soups. Here they're made with Manchego, Spanish sheep's-milk cheese. Parmesan or cheddar work as well.

PREP 15 minutes **COOK** 9 minutes

1 cup shredded Manchego cheese
   (4 ounces)
3 tablespoons olive oil
3 tablespoons balsamic vinegar
¼ teaspoon kosher salt
¼ teaspoon freshly ground black pepper
3 cups strawberries, halved and/or
   quartered
4 cups baby arugula

1. For each frico: Heat a medium nonstick skillet over medium heat. Sprinkle one-third of the cheese on the bottom of the skillet, shaking the skillet so cheese is in an even layer. Cook for 2 to 3 minutes or until cheese starts to bubble and browns around the edges. Remove skillet from heat for 30 to 40 seconds or until cheese is set. Using a spatula and fork, carefully turn frico over, return to heat and cook for 1 to 2 minutes more or until underside is golden. Slide frico out of pan onto a wire rack.

2. For salad: In a large bowl, combine olive oil, balsamic vinegar, salt and pepper. Add strawberries and arugula; toss to coat. Divide among six serving plates or serve on a large platter.

3. Break fricos into pieces and serve with salad. **Makes 6 servings.**

Per serving: 165 cal, 13 g fat, 17 mg chol, 192 mg sodium, 8 g carbo, 2 g fiber, 6 g pro.

Asian Cabbage Salad

PREP 25 minutes **CHILL** 30 minutes

Peanut Butter Dressing (recipe follows)
6 cups packaged shredded cabbage with
   carrot (coleslaw mix)
1 cup fresh sugar snap peas, trimmed and
   thinly sliced lengthwise
½ cup coarsely shredded, peeled jicama
¼ cup thinly sliced green onion (2)
¼ cup sliced almonds, toasted*
   Fresh cilantro (optional)

1. Prepare Peanut Butter Dressing. Toss shredded cabbage, peas, jicama and green onion with the dressing. Cover and chill for 30 to 60 minutes.

2. Just before serving, sprinkle with toasted almonds and, if you like, cilantro. **Makes 6 to 8 servings.**

*Note: To toast nuts, spread them in a small dry skillet and heat over medium heat just until lightly toasted. Stir frequently and watch carefully so nuts don't burn.

Peanut Butter Dressing: In a large bowl, combine ⅓ cup creamy peanut butter; 1 teaspoon curry powder; and ½ teaspoon each salt, garlic powder and ground ginger. Gradually whisk in ⅓ cup water, 2 tablespoons lemon juice and 2 tablespoons olive oil until smooth.

Per serving: 176 cal, 14 g fat, 0 mg chol, 277 mg sodium, 10 g carbo, 3 g fiber, 6 g pro.

Strawberry Balsamic Dressing

The sweet tang of this rosy dressing pairs nicely with nuts, cheese, avocado or grilled chicken breast in a mixed green salad.

START TO FINISH 15 minutes

2 cups chopped fresh or frozen (thawed) chopped strawberries
⅓ cup olive oil
2 tablespoons white balsamic vinegar or balsamic vinegar
1 tablespoon packed brown sugar
¼ teaspoon kosher salt
¾ teaspoon ground black pepper

In a blender or food processor, combine all ingredients. Cover and blend or process until smooth. Store, covered, in the refrigerator for up to 3 days. Whisk well before serving. **Makes 1¾ cups.**

Per 2 tablespoons: 60 cal, 5 g fat, 0 g chol, 36 mg sodium, 4 g carbo, 0 g fiber, 0 g pro.

Buttermilk Pesto Dressing

Try this creamy blend on a green salad with chicken or shrimp, or use it in a pasta salad with cherry tomatoes. We also like it drizzled over grilled or steamed asparagus.

PREP 10 minutes **CHILL** 2 hours

½ cup buttermilk
¼ cup fat-free plain Greek yogurt
¼ cup light mayonnaise
4 teaspoons prepared basil pesto
½ teaspoon ground black pepper

In a medium bowl, whisk together all the ingredients. Cover and chill for at least 2 hours or up to 24 hours. Whisk before serving. **Makes 1 cup.**

Per 2 tablespoons: 47 cal, 4 g fat, 4 mg chol, 92 mg sodium, 2 g carbo, 0 g fiber, 2 g pro.

Asian Vinaigrette

Toss this light soy-ginger dressing with a bag of slaw mix and roasted peanuts for a nutritious side dish on stir-fry night.

START TO FINISH 10 minutes

⅓ cup rice vinegar
¼ cup canola oil
1 tablespoon packed brown sugar
2 tablespoons toasted sesame oil
2 tablespoons water
1 tablespoon low-sodium soy sauce
1 tablespoon grated fresh ginger
½ teaspoon Dijon-style mustard

In a blender or food processor, combine all ingredients. Cover and blend or process until smooth. Store, covered, in the refrigerator for up to 5 days. Shake or whisk well before serving. (The dressing separates quickly.) **Makes 1 cup.**

Per 2 tablespoons: 104 cal, 10 g fat, 0 g chol, 80 mg sodium, 6 g carbo, 0 g fiber, 0 g pro.

The herd of the Uplands Cheese Company in southern Wisconsin enjoys the warm breeze and fresh green pasture. The evening milk the cows produce—rich with more fat than milk given any other time of day—will be turned into buttery Pleasant Ridge Reserve, one of the most-awarded cheeses in the history of American cheese-making.

ASIAN VINAIGRETTE

BUTTERMILK PESTO
DRESSING

STRAWBERRY BALSAMIC
DRESSING

HERBED POTATO SALAD

GRILLED VEGETABLES WITH SUMMER HOLLANDAISE

Herbed Potato Salad

Olive oil and vinegar thin the dressing in this creamy potato salad. Garnish with your favorite fresh herbs to add even more flavor.

PREP 15 minutes **COOK** 15 minutes

- 3 pounds small red potatoes, unpeeled and cut into 1½-inch chunks
- 3 tablespoons extra virgin olive oil
- 2 tablespoons cider vinegar
- 1 tablespoon fresh herbs (such as snipped tarragon, dill or parsley)
- 2 tablespoons sour cream
- 2 tablespoons mayonnaise
- 2 teaspoons Dijon-style mustard
- 1 green onion, chopped
- 1 teaspoon salt
- ½ teaspoon ground black pepper
- ¼ teaspoon celery seeds (optional)

1. For potatoes: Place steamer basket in a large saucepan. Add water to reach just below bottom of basket; heat until simmering. Add potatoes to basket. Cover; reduce to medium heat. Steam for 15 to 18 minutes or until potatoes are fork-tender. Remove from heat. Cool slightly.

2. Meanwhile, in a large bowl, combine remaining ingredients, (If you like, add celery seeds.) Add potatoes; toss gently to combine. Serve potato salad warm or cool. **Makes 8 servings.**

Make-ahead directions: Chill, covered, up to 4 hours. Let stand 20 minutes at room temperature before serving.

Per serving: 195 cal, 8 g fat, 3 mg chol, 375 mg sodium, 27 g carbo, 3 g fiber, 3 g pro.

Grilled Vegetables

Grilling asparagus and Broccolini over dry heat concentrates their sweetness and adds a delectable smoky flavor.

PREP 10 minutes **GRILL** 3 minutes

- 3 pounds fresh asparagus spears and/or Broccolini, trimmed
- 2 tablespoons olive oil
- ½ teaspoon salt
- ¼ teaspoon ground black pepper
  Summer Hollandaise (see recipe, right)

1. Snap off and discard woody bases from asparagus. Spread asparagus and/or Broccolini on two large baking pans. Drizzle with oil. Sprinkle with salt and pepper. Turn to coat.

2. For a charcoal or gas grill, place vegetables on grill perpendicular to bars of grill grate over medium heat. Grill, covered, just until tender, 3 to 5 minutes, turning once. Transfer to a platter. Serve with Summer Hollandaise. **Makes 8 servings.**

Oven method: Transfer roasting pan with coated vegetables to a 400° oven. Roast, uncovered, about 15 minutes or until crisp-tender, turning once.

Make-ahead directions: Vegetables can be grilled ahead, covered and chilled. Serve at room temperature.

Per serving: 200 cal, 17 g fat, 100 mg chol, 425 mg sodium, 10 g carbo, 4 g fiber, 5 g pro.

Summer Hollandaise

Making this sauce in a blender means there's no fear of it separating.

START TO FINISH 10 minutes

- 3 pasteurized egg yolks
- ½ of a lemon, juiced
- ½ teaspoon salt
  Pinch mustard powder
  Pinch ground white pepper (optional)
- ½ cup butter, melted
- 1 teaspoon snipped fresh tarragon leaves
  Grilled Vegetables (see recipe, left)

In a blender or small food processor, combine egg yolks, lemon juice, salt, mustard powder and, if you like, white pepper. Cover; blend or process until smooth. With machine running, drizzle in melted butter until sauce thickens. Add tarragon; blend just until chopped. Transfer to a small saucepan and gently heat over low heat for 2 to 4 minutes or until warm. Serve with Grilled Vegetables (see recipe, left). **Makes 8 servings.**

Make-ahead directions: Chill sauce up to 8 hours; gently reheat before serving.

Per serving: 124 cal, 13 g fat, 100 mg chol, 250 mg sodium, 1 g carbo, 0 g fiber, 1 g pro.

CHAI-SPICED COMPOTE

GREEN TEA ICE CREAM

Chai-Spiced Compote

Chai tea bags infuse this healthy dessert with the tongue-tingling ginger, cloves and cardamom.

PREP 15 minutes **COOK** 7 minutes
STAND 5 minutes

  1 cup water
½ cup sugar
  4 chai tea bags or spiced citrus tea bags
  3 cups frozen unsweetened peach slices
  2 cups frozen unsweetened pitted dark
    sweet cherries
  2 teaspoons brandy or 1 teaspoon vanilla
    Flaked coconut, toasted*
    Pecans, chopped and toasted (see tip,
      page 39)
    Pound cake (optional)

1. In a medium saucepan, combine the water and sugar. Bring to boiling, stirring to dissolve sugar; reduce heat. Simmer, covered, for 5 minutes. Remove saucepan from heat. Add tea bags; cover and let stand for 5 minutes. Discard tea bags.

2. Add peaches to tea mixture. Return to boiling; reduce heat. Simmer, uncovered, about 2 minutes or until peaches are tender.

3. Transfer the peach mixture to a medium bowl. Stir in the frozen cherries and brandy. Let cool slightly or chill, covered, for at least 6 hours or overnight. Serve with coconut, pecans and, if you like, pound cake. **Makes 4 to 6 servings.**

*Tip: To toast coconut, spread coconut in a shallow baking pan. Bake in a 350° oven for 5 to 10 minutes or until lightly browned, shaking the pan once or twice. Watch carefully so coconut doesn't burn.

Per serving: 273 cal, 6 g fat, 0 mg chol, 15 mg sodium, 3 g carbo, 5 g fiber, 3 g pro.

Green Tea Ice Cream

Look for matcha, or powdered green tea, at specialty stores or online. It looks a little like eye shadow and gives this ice cream its gorgeous color and subtle tea flavor.

PREP 20 minutes **STAND** 20 minutes
FREEZE 9 hours

    2 cups half-and-half or light cream
    1 tablespoon matcha (100% natural
        powdered green tea)
    1¼ cups sugar
    1 tablespoon vanilla
    ⅛ teaspoon salt
    2 cups whipping cream
        Creme-filled, rolled wafer cookies
        (optional)

1. In a small saucepan, heat 1 cup of the half-and-half just until it comes to a simmer; remove from heat. Stir in matcha. Let the mixture stand at room temperature for 20 minutes.

2. In a large mixing bowl, combine the remaining half-and-half, the sugar, vanilla and salt. Stir until sugar dissolves. Stir whipping cream and matcha mixture into the sugar mixture.

3. Transfer mixture to a 9x9x2-inch baking pan. Cover with foil. Freeze for 3 to 4 hours or until partially frozen.

4. Remove pan from the freezer; break mixture into chunks and transfer to a chilled large bowl. Beat ice cream chunks with an electric mixer on low to medium-low speed for 2 to 3 minutes or until mixture is smooth. Return mixture to the cold 9x9x2-inch baking pan. Cover and freeze for 6 hours or until firm. Serve in chilled bowls and, if you like, garnish with cookies. **Makes 12 servings.**

Per ½ cup: 323 cal, 20 g fat, 70 mg chol, 83 mg sodium, 34 g carbo, 0 g fiber, 3 g pro.

Vanilla Flan with Butterscotch Sauce

For the butterscotch sauce, simply press the brown sugar, with a pinch of salt, in the bottom of the dish. It dissolves into a sauce as the flan bakes and chills.

PREP 25 minutes **BAKE** 35 minutes **COOL** 30 minutes **CHILL** 6 hours

    3 cups half-and-half
    1 vanilla bean or 2 teaspoons vanilla extract
    ½ cup packed brown sugar
    ½ teaspoon salt
    5 eggs
    ½ cup granulated sugar

1. In a medium saucepan, heat half-and-half and vanilla bean over medium heat until steaming (140° to 145°), about 3 minutes (too hot to insert a finger for more than a moment). Remove from heat; cover. Steep for 15 minutes.

2. Position rack in lower third of oven; preheat oven to 350°. In a small bowl, combine brown sugar and ¼ teaspoon of the salt, pinching and mashing brown sugar to eliminate lumps. Spoon mixture into a 9-inch deep-dish pie plate. Pack into a firm, even layer.

3. Remove vanilla bean from half-and-half (let cool if too hot to handle); cut bean in half lengthwise. With the point of a small knife, scrape seeds from bean and add to half-and-half. Reheat mixture for 1 to 2 minutes, just to steaming.

4. In a large bowl, whisk eggs, granulated sugar and the remaining ¼ teaspoon salt. Gradually whisk in warm half-and-half until well combined.

5. Slowly pour egg mixture over brown sugar into pie plate. Some sugar may float up but will settle to bottom eventually.

6. Place pie plate in a deep roasting pan. Place pan on rack positioned in lower third of a 350° oven. Pour boiling water in roasting pan to halfway up sides of pie plate. Bake for 35 to 40 minutes or until a knife inserted in center comes out clean.

7. Carefully remove pie plate from roasting pan. Cool on wire rack for 30 minutes. Refrigerate, covered, at least 6 hours or overnight. To serve, gently run a thin metal spatula or knife around edge of flan. Invert onto serving plate. **Makes 8 servings.**

Per serving: 282 cal, 13 g fat, 165 mg chol, 231 mg sodium, 35 g carbo, 0 g fiber, 7 g pro.

Chocolate-Marshmallow Ice Cream Sandwiches

PREP 45 minutes **FREEZE** 4 hours
BAKE 10 minutes per batch **STAND** 10 minutes

10 miniature caramel Twix bars
 1 2-layer-size chocolate cake mix
 2 eggs
 ¼ cup vegetable oil
 ¼ cup water
 2 cups chocolate ice cream
 ⅔ cup marshmallow creme

1. Unwrap Twix bars; place in resealable plastic bag. Seal and freeze for 2 hours.

2. Meanwhile, for cookies: In a large mixing bowl, combine cake mix, eggs, oil and water. Beat with electric mixer until combined. Drop dough by well-rounded teaspoons onto ungreased cookie sheets. Bake in a 350° oven about 10 minutes or until tops are set. Cool for 1 minute on cookie sheets. Transfer cookies to wire racks; cool completely.

3. Spoon ice cream into a large bowl. Let stand about 10 minutes to soften slightly. Meanwhile, using the flat side of a meat mallet or a rolling pin, crush frozen Twix bars. Stir into ice cream; return to freezer until ready to use.

4. Spread marshmallow creme on flat sides of half of the cookies; place, creme sides up, on a shallow baking pan. Using a small ice cream scoop, place some ice cream mixture onto flat sides of remaining cookies. Place on same baking pan, ice cream sides up. Loosely cover and freeze for 2 hours or until firm.

5. Gently sandwich cookies together. Serve immediately or wrap each sandwich in plastic wrap and freeze in freezer container up to 1 month. **Makes about 14 sandwiches.**

Per sandwich: 288 cal, 11 g fat, 37 mg chol, 292 mg sodium, 45 g carbo, 1 g fiber, 4 g pro.

Choose-a-Fruit Fool

No one knows how fools (a centuries-old blend of whipped cream and fruit) got their playful name. Maybe it's because with just four ingredients, you'd be foolish not to make one!

PREP 30 minutes **STAND** 10 minutes **CHILL** 2 hours

1½ cups fruit (raspberries, blackberries, blueberries, thinly sliced strawberries or peeled and finely chopped peaches, mangoes, apricots or kiwifruits)
 1 to 2 tablespoons sugar
 1 cup whipping cream
 2 tablespoons sugar
 ½ teaspoon vanilla
    Additional fruit (optional)
    Cookies (optional)

1. For fruit: In a large bowl, combine the fruit and 1 to 2 tablespoons sugar, to taste. Let stand for 10 minutes. In a food processor or blender, puree 1 cup of the fruit mixture. Stir pureed fruit back into the fruit in the bowl. Cover and chill about 2 hours or until cold.

2. For cream: In a chilled mixing bowl, combine whipping cream, 2 tablespoons sugar and the vanilla. Using chilled beaters, beat with an electric mixer on medium speed until nearly stiff peaks form.

3. With a rubber spatula, gently fold the chilled fruit mixture into the whipped cream, leaving ribbons of fruit. (Do not overmix.) To serve, divide the swirled fool among six small glasses. If you like, garnish with fruit and serve with cookies. **Makes 6 servings.**

Per serving: 244 cal, 17 g fat, 56 g chol, 52 mg sodium, 22 g carbo, 4 g fiber, 2 g pro.

Rhubarb Fool: In a small saucepan, bring ⅓ cup sugar, 1 tablespoon water, 1 tablespoon finely snipped crystallized ginger and a strip of orange peel to boiling. Stir in 1½ cups sliced rhubarb (thawed, if frozen). Return to boiling; reduce heat. Simmer, covered, over low heat for 10 to 12 minutes or until fruit is very tender. Remove orange peel. If you like, stir in a drop of red food coloring; cool to room temperature. In a food processor or blender, puree rhubarb, then cover and chill until cold. Continue as directed in Step 2.

RHUBARB FOOL AND
BLACKBERRY FOOL

Best-Ever Strawberry-Rhubarb Pie

Yummy strawberry-rhubarb pie filling gets a spark of spicy ginger flavor, then goes into a remarkably easy slice-and-bake crust.

PREP 45 minutes **FREEZE** 1 hour **STAND** 15 minutes **BAKE** 1 hour 15 minutes

Rich Butter Pastry (recipe follows)
1¼ cups sugar
2½ tablespoons quick-cooking tapioca
1 tablespoon grated fresh ginger
¼ teaspoon salt
1 pound fresh rhubarb, cut into 1-inch pieces (3 cups), or one 16-ounce package frozen cut rhubarb
3 cups sliced fresh strawberries

1. Prepare Rich Butter Pastry.

2. For strawberry-rhubarb filling: In a large bowl, stir together sugar, tapioca, ginger and salt. Add rhubarb and strawberries; gently toss until coated. Let rhubarb mixture stand for 15 minutes, stirring occasionally. (If using frozen rhubarb, let mixture stand 45 minutes.) Meanwhile, remove pastry from freezer and let stand 10 to 15 minutes or until easy to slice.

3. Using a sharp knife with a thin blade, cut the chilled 7-inch pastry log into 28 thin slices. Place 16 of the slices around the edge of a 9-inch deep-dish pie plate. Place the remaining slices in the bottom of the pie plate. Using your fingers, press the pieces of the pastry together to fill in the gaps. Flute edge as desired.

4. Stir fruit mixture and transfer to the pastry-lined pie plate. Slice the remaining pastry into 15 to 18 slices. Place slices on top of fruit.

5. To prevent overbrowning, cover edge of pie with foil. Place a foil-lined baking sheet on the rack below the pie in oven. Bake in a 375° oven for 60 minutes (75 minutes if using frozen fruit). Remove foil; bake for 15 to 20 minutes more or until filling is bubbly and crust is golden. Cool on a wire rack. **Makes 8 servings.**

Rich Butter Pastry: In a medium bowl, stir together 2¼ cups all-purpose flour, ¼ cup sugar and ¼ teaspoon salt. Using a pastry blender, cut in ½ cup shortening and ¼ cup cold butter, cut into cubes, until pieces are pea-size. Sprinkle 1 tablespoon cold water over part of the flour mixture; toss with a fork. Push moistened pastry to side of bowl. Repeat moistening flour mixture, using 1 tablespoon cold water at a time, until all the flour mixture is moistened (6 to 7 tablespoons water total). Gather flour mixture into a ball, using hands to combine until it holds together. Divide pastry into two portions, one portion with one-third of the dough and one portion with two-thirds of the dough. Shape the small piece of pastry into a 5x1½-inch round log. Shape the large piece of dough into a 7x2-inch round log. Wrap pastry with plastic wrap and freeze for 1 to 2 hours or until firm.

Per serving: 481 cal, 19 g fat, 15 mg chol, 201 mg sodium, 74 g carbo, 3 g fiber, 5 g pro.

Blueberry Cheesecake Cupcakes

PREP 30 minutes **BAKE** 20 minutes **COOL** 1 hour

1 package 2-layer-size yellow cake mix
1 4-serving-size package cheesecake instant pudding and pie filling mix
3 eggs
1 cup water
¼ cup vegetable oil
½ of an 8-ounce package cream cheese, cut into small pieces and softened
⅔ cup fresh or frozen blueberries, lightly mashed
½ cup graham cracker crumbs
2 4-serving-size packages cheesecake instant pudding and pie filling mix
2 cups whipping cream
1 cup milk
Graham cracker crumbs
1 cup blueberry pie filling, blueberry preserves or blueberry spreadable fruit

1. Line twenty-four 2½-inch muffin cups with paper bake cups; set aside.

2. In a large mixing bowl, beat cake mix, one package of pudding mix, eggs, the water and oil on low speed until combined. Beat on medium to high speed for 2 minutes more (batter will be thick). Fold in cream cheese pieces and blueberries.

3. Divide batter among muffin cups, filling cups two-thirds full and smoothing tops. Sprinkle with the ½ cup graham cracker crumbs.

4. Bake in a 350° oven for 20 to 25 minutes or until a wooden toothpick inserted in centers comes out clean. Cool in pans on a wire rack for 5 minutes. Remove from muffin cups. Cool completely on wire racks.

5. In a medium mixing bowl, whisk together the two packages of instant pudding mix, whipping cream and milk until the mixture is thickened.

6. Spread or pipe frosting on cupcakes. Use the back of a spoon to make a shallow depression in the frosting. Sprinkle with additional graham cracker crumbs, then spoon a rounded teaspoon of blueberry pie filling into each depression. Store, chilled, in airtight container for up to 3 days. **Makes 22 to 24 cupcakes.**

Per cupcake: 266 cal, 15 g fat, 57 mg chol, 370 mg sodium, 30 g carbo, 1 g fiber, 3 g pro.

Malt Shop Special Cupcakes

PREP 25 minutes **BAKE** 18 minutes **COOL** 1 hour

1 package 2-layer-size German chocolate cake mix
1 cup water
⅓ cup vegetable oil
3 eggs
¼ cup malted milk powder
2 4-serving-size packages vanilla instant pudding and pie filling mix
4 cups whipping cream
1 cup malted milk powder
⅔ cup chopped malted milk balls
⅓ cup hot fudge ice cream topping, warmed
18 to 20 maraschino cherries with stems, drained and patted dry

1. Line twenty 2½-inch muffin cups with paper bake cups; set aside.

2. In a large mixing bowl, beat cake mix, the water, oil, eggs and the ¼ cup malted milk powder with an electric mixer on low speed until combined. Beat on medium speed for 2 minutes more.

3. Divide batter among prepared muffin cups, filling cups two-thirds full.

4. Bake in a 350° oven about 18 minutes or until a wooden toothpick inserted in centers comes out clean. Cool cupcakes in muffin cups on wire racks for 5 minutes. Remove cupcakes from muffin cups. Cool completely on wire racks.

5. For frosting, in a large mixing bowl, beat the pudding mixes, whipping cream and the 1 cup malted milk powder with an electric mixer on medium speed until stiff peaks form. Pipe or spread frosting over cupcakes. Sprinkle with malted milk balls, drizzle with fudge topping and top with a cherry. Store, chilled, in an airtight container for up to 2 days. **Makes 18 to 20 cupcakes.**

Per cupcake: 529 cal, 30 g fat, 110 mg chol, 529 mg sodium, 59 g carbo, 1 g fiber, 7 g pro.

In a pinch, you can pipe frosting with a resealable plastic bag that has one corner snipped off, but you'll get more control and prettier swirls with a pastry bag and tips. Worried about cleanup? Use disposable bags.

MALT SHOP
SPECIAL

ROOT BEER
FLOAT

BLUEBERRY
CHEESECAKE

Root Beer Float Cupcakes

(Pictured on page 51.)

PREP 40 minutes **BAKE** 12 minutes
COOL 1 hour **CHILL** 30 minutes

  1 package 2-layer-size yellow cake mix
  3 eggs
  1 cup root beer
  ⅓ cup vegetable oil
  4½ teaspoons root beer flavoring
  2 teaspoons root beer flavoring
  1 12- to 16-ounce container rich and creamy
     buttercream frosting
  22 to 24 root beer-flavor hard candy barrels
  24 bendable straws

1. Line twenty-two to twenty-four 2½-inch muffin cups with paper bake cups; set aside.

2. In a large mixing bowl, beat cake mix, eggs, root beer, oil and the 4½ teaspoons root beer flavoring on low speed until combined. Beat on medium to high speed for 2 minutes more (batter will be thick).

3. Divide batter among prepared muffin cups, filling cups two-thirds full.

4. Bake in a 350° oven 12 to 15 minutes or until a wooden toothpick inserted in centers comes out clean. Cool in muffin cups on wire racks for 5 minutes. Remove from cups. Cool completely on racks.

5. Meanwhile, in a small bowl, stir the 2 teaspoons root beer flavoring into the buttercream frosting.

6. To make the frosting look like ice cream, chill to firm slightly, then scoop a small amount onto each cupcake. Chill cupcakes for at least 30 minutes before serving.

7. Just before serving, top each cupcake with a root beer candy. Cut straws in half; discard bottom (straight) halves. Garnish each cupcake with a bent straw half.
Makes 22 to 24 cupcakes.

Per cupcake: 246 cal, 9 g fat, 26 mg chol, 203 mg sodium, 40 g carbo, 0 g fiber, 2 g pro.

Peach Cordial Mini Bundt Cakes

These petite cakes are perfect for a bridal or baby shower.

PREP 35 minutes **BAKE** 20 minutes **COOL** 1 hour

  ½ cup peach nectar
  ½ cup rum
  ¾ cup unsalted butter, softened
  1¼ cups granulated sugar
  2 eggs
  ½ teaspoon almond extract
  ½ teaspoon vanilla
  1½ cups unbleached all-purpose flour
  1½ teaspoons baking powder
  1 teaspoon kosher salt
  ½ teaspoon baking soda
  ½ cup boiling water
  2 cups powdered sugar
  ¼ cup unsalted butter, melted

1. Butter and flour six 1-cup fluted individual tube pans or eight 3¼-inch muffin cups; set aside. In a glass measuring cup, combine peach nectar and rum; set aside.

2. In a large mixing bowl, beat ½ cup of the softened butter with an electric mixer on medium speed for 30 seconds. Add 1 cup of the granulated sugar; beat for 2 minutes. Add eggs, one at a time, beating well after each. Beat in the almond extract and vanilla. Sift the flour, baking powder, kosher salt and baking soda into the batter. Beat just until combined. Add ½ cup of the rum mixture and the boiling water. Stir by hand until the liquids are incorporated. Divide batter evenly among prepared pans.

3. Bake in a 350° oven for 20 to 25 minutes for the fluted individual tube pans or 18 to 20 minutes for the muffin cups or until a wooden toothpick inserted near centers comes out clean.

4. Meanwhile, for syrup: In a saucepan, combine ¼ cup of the remaining rum mixture with the remaining ¼ cup granulated sugar and ¼ cup softened butter. Cook and stir until sugar dissolves and mixture just comes to a simmer.

5. Place cakes in pans on a wire rack. Poke about a dozen holes in each cake with a toothpick. Slowly and evenly spoon syrup over cakes. Cool in pans about 1 hour or until cakes absorb syrup. Unmold cakes.

6. For icing: In a medium bowl, briskly stir the remaining ¼ cup rum mixture, the powdered sugar and ¼ cup melted butter. Drizzle over cakes. **Makes 6 mini cakes.**

Per mini cake: 784 cal, 33 g fat, 143 mg chol, 555 mg sodium, 109 g carbo, 1 g fiber, 6 g pro.

PEACH CORDIAL
MINI BUNDT CAKES

GOOEY
BUTTER BARS

Gooey Butter Bars

These bars are a blank canvas for whatever topping you like. We piled on strawberries tossed with a little honey and minced ginger.

PREP 25 minutes **BAKE** 30 minutes

1½ cups all-purpose flour
¼ cup sugar
½ cup cold butter
⅔ cup butter, softened
1¼ cups sugar
¼ cup light-color corn syrup
1 egg
½ teaspoon almond extract
1 cup all-purpose flour
⅔ cup half-and-half
3 cups sliced or halved fresh strawberries
2 tablespoons honey
1 teaspoon grated fresh ginger

1. Line a 13x9x2-inch baking pan with parchment; set aside.

2. For crust: In a medium bowl, combine the 1½ cups flour and ¼ cup sugar. Using a pastry blender, cut in the ½ cup butter until mixture resembles fine crumbs. Pat into prepared pan; set aside.

3. In a large mixing bowl, beat softened butter with an electric mixer on medium-high speed for 30 seconds. Gradually beat in the 1¼ cups sugar. Beat in corn syrup, egg and almond extract Alternately add flour and half-and-half, beating after each addition just until combined (batter may appear slightly curdled). Gently spread over crust in pan.

4. Bake in a 350° oven about 30 minutes or just until center is set. Cool in pan on wire rack. Use parchment to lift uncut bars from pan; cut into bars. In a small bowl, toss strawberries with honey and ginger; serve with bars. **Makes 24 bars.**

Per bar: 209 cal, 10 g fat, 34 mg chol, 88 mg sodium, 29 g carbo, 2 g pro.

Raspberry and Vanilla Stack Cakes

Layers of raspberry jelly and raspberry cream elevate humble sponge cake to a lovely treat for company. To easily cut sponge cake into layers, cover the cake with plastic wrap and freeze 2 hours before slicing.

PREP 40 minutes **BAKE** 30 minutes **COOL** 2 hours

1½ cups all-purpose flour
1½ teaspoons baking powder
½ teaspoon salt
3 eggs, room temperature
1½ cups sugar
¾ cup milk
3 tablespoons butter
2 teaspoons vanilla bean paste or vanilla extract
1¼ cups whipping cream
⅔ cup raspberry or cherry jelly
Powdered sugar

1. Grease and flour a 13x9x2-inch baking pan. Line the bottom of pan with waxed paper; set aside. In a bowl, stir together flour, baking powder and salt; set aside.

2. In a medium mixing bowl, beat eggs with an electric mixer on high speed about 4 minutes or until thick. Gradually add sugar, beating on medium speed 4 to 5 minutes or until light and fluffy. Add flour mixture; beat on low to medium speed just until combined.

3. In a small saucepan, heat and stir milk and butter until butter is melted. Add to batter along with the vanilla paste; beat until combined. Pour batter into prepared pan, spreading evenly.

4. Bake in a 350° oven for 30 to 35 minutes or until a wooden toothpick inserted near center comes out clean. Cool cake in pan on a wire rack for 15 minutes. Remove cake from pan; peel off waxed paper. Place cake on a baking sheet. Cover with plastic wrap; cool completely.

5. In a chilled large mixing bowl, beat whipping cream with an electric mixer on medium speed until soft peaks form. Gradually add ⅓ cup of the jelly. Beat until combined.

6. Using a serrated knife, trim cake edges to create straight sides. Cut cake lengthwise in half. Cut each half into seven 4¼x1¾-inch pieces. (You should have 14 mini cakes.) Split cakes horizontally into three layers. For each cake, spread a thin layer of remaining jelly on the bottom cake layer; top with 1 tablespoon whipped cream mixture. Add second cake layer; repeat jelly and whipped cream steps. Finish with top cake layer. Sprinkle with powdered sugar. **Makes 14 cakes.**

Per cake: 295 cal, 12 g fat, 77 mg chol, 179 mg sodium, 45 g carbo, 1 g fiber, 4 g pro.

Salted Caramel, Chocolate and Peanut Cracker-Stack Bars

What's a Midwest party without bars? This recipe is a twist on old-fashioned cracker bars.
They cut beautifully and serve a crowd.

PREP 30 minutes **CHILL** 2 hours

  8 ounces rich rectangular crackers
  ¾ cup butter
  ¾ cup honey
  1 cup packed brown sugar
  ⅓ cup whipping cream
  2 cups finely crushed graham crackers
  1 teaspoon vanilla
  ½ teaspoon fine sea salt
  2 cups chocolate-covered peanut butter
      cups, chopped into ½-inch pieces
      (9 ounces)
  2 cups dry-roasted peanuts
  1½ cups milk chocolate pieces (9 ounces)
  ⅓ cup butterscotch-flavor pieces
  ⅓ cup creamy peanut butter

1. Line a 13x9x2-inch baking pan with nonstick foil, extending foil over the edges of the pan. Arrange half of the crackers in a single layer over bottom of prepared pan.

2. For caramel: In a medium saucepan, combine butter, honey, brown sugar and cream. Bring to boiling, stirring constantly. Add graham cracker crumbs, reduce heat to a simmer and continue to cook mixture for 5 minutes, stirring constantly. Remove from heat and stir in vanilla and ¼ teaspoon of the sea salt.

3. Pour half of the caramel over the cracker layer in pan, spreading to cover. Sprinkle with chopped peanut butter cups and peanuts. Pour remaining caramel over peanut butter cups and peanuts. Arrange remaining crackers in a single layer on top of caramel layer, pushing slightly to secure.

4. In a medium microwave-safe bowl, combine chocolate and butterscotch pieces. Microwave for 2 to 3 minutes or until melted, stirring every 30 seconds. Stir in peanut butter until smooth. Spread chocolate mixture over cracker layer; immediately sprinkle with remaining ¼ teaspoon sea salt.

5. Chill bars for 2 hours or until very firm. Using the edges of the foil, lift the uncut bars out of the pan. Cut into bars.
Makes 32 to 40 bars.

Per bar: 346 cal, 20 g fat, 19 mg chol, 220 mg sodium, 38 g carbo, 2 g fiber, 5 g pro.

There are few better ways to spend a spring afternoon than kicking off your shoes and climbing an easy tree. Such a perch provides a nice view of all of that beautiful green!

**TOMATO PASTA WITH
ARUGULA AND PARMESAN,
PAGE 100**

Summer

Fresh Vegetable Chips

These chips are a fresh and playful take on the traditional potato chips—and a whole lot more healthy.

START TO FINISH 30 minutes

1 bunch large red radishes, trimmed (12 ounces)
1 small jicama, peeled
1 large daikon, peeled
1 teaspoon smoked paprika
1¼ teaspoons salt
¼ teaspoon sugar
¼ teaspoon ground black pepper
4 teaspoons lime zest
   Caramelized Onion Dip (see recipe, right) (optional)

1. Slice radishes, jicama and daikon about ¼ inch thick. Halve large slices of jicama. Transfer vegetables to platter.

2. In a small bowl, combine smoked paprika, salt, sugar, pepper and lime zest.

3. To serve, sprinkle paprika mixture over vegetables. Serve with Caramelized Onion Dip, if you like. **Makes 8 servings.**

Make-ahead directions: Cover chips; chill up to 8 hours.

Per serving: 37 cal, 0 g fat, 0 g chol, 389 mg sodium, 8 g carbo, 4 g fiber, 1 g pro.

Caramelized Onion Dip

If the onions begin to stick as they cook, add a little bit of water to the pan.

PREP 20 minutes   **COOK** 15 minutes   **CHILL** 1 hour

2 tablespoons olive oil
2 cups chopped onions (2 large)
2 teaspoons sugar
1 teaspoon salt
4 cloves garlic, minced
1½ cups light sour cream
⅔ cup light mayonnaise
¼ teaspoon ground black pepper
   Fresh Vegetable Chips (see recipe, left)

1. In a large skillet, heat olive oil over medium heat. Add onions, sugar and ½ teaspoon of the salt; toss to mix. Reduce heat to medium-low. Cook and stir onions for 15 to 20 minutes or until golden. Remove from heat; let cool. Stir in garlic.

2. In a medium bowl, combine the cooled onion mixture, sour cream, mayonnaise, the remaining ½ teaspoon salt and the pepper. Chill, covered, at least 1 hour to let flavors blend.

3. Transfer to a serving bowl; stir. Serve dip with Fresh Vegetable Chips. **Makes 8 servings (1⅓ cups).**

Make-ahead directions: Cover and chill for up to 24 hours before serving. Let stand about 20 minutes at room temperature before serving.

Per 2 tablespoons: 147 cal, 12 g fat, 16 mg chol, 467 mg sodium, 10 g carbo, 1 g fiber, 1 g pro.

Blue Cheese and Bacon Mini Corn Dogs

Bacon and blue cheese stud the crackly cornmeal crust of these pint-size appetizers. Serve with homemade Blue Cheese Dip or prepared honey mustard.

PREP 30 minutes **FRY** 2 minutes per batch

    1 cup all-purpose flour
    ⅔ cup yellow cornmeal
    2 tablespoons sugar
    1½ teaspoons baking powder
    ½ teaspoon dry mustard
    ¼ teaspoon salt
    1 tablespoon shortening
    ¾ cup milk
    ¼ cup crumbled blue cheese
    1 egg
    3 slices bacon, crisp-cooked and finely
        crumbled or chopped
    Oil for deep-frying
    12 6-inch wooden skewers
    6 jumbo beef hot dogs, cut in half crosswise
    Honey mustard or mustard
    Blue Cheese Dip (recipe follows) (optional)
    Fresh Italian (flat-leaf) parsley

1. In a large bowl, combine flour, cornmeal, sugar, baking powder, dry mustard and salt. Cut in the shortening until mixture resembles fine crumbs. In a blender, combine milk, blue cheese and egg; cover and blend until almost smooth. Add egg mixture to flour mixture along with bacon; mix well. (Batter will be thick.)

2. Meanwhile, heat 1 inch of oil in a heavy large skillet over medium heat to 365° (should take about 15 minutes).

3. Insert skewers into ends of hot dogs. Holding on to skewers, hold hot dogs over bowl of cornmeal mixture. Spoon cornmeal mixture on hot dogs and spread to completely cover. Place coated hot dogs, three or four at a time, on their sides in hot oil. Turn hot dogs with tongs after about 10 seconds of cooking to prevent batter from sliding off. Cook for 2 to 3 minutes more or until golden brown, turning to brown evenly. Remove and drain on a baking sheet lined with paper towels.

Keep warm in a 200° oven while frying remaining hot dogs. Serve warm with honey mustard and, if you like, Blue Cheese Dip. Sprinkle with parsley. **Makes 12 appetizer corn dogs.**

Blue Cheese Dip: In a medium bowl, combine ⅔ cup mayonnaise, ¼ cup sour cream, 2 ounces crumbled blue cheese, 1 teaspoon Worcestershire sauce and ⅛ teaspoon ground black pepper. Cover and chill until ready to serve.

Per corn dog: 259 cal, 15 g fat, 49 mg chol, 564 mg sodium, 23 g carbo, 1 g fiber, 9 g pro.

Bring the flavors and fun of the state fair home with these seasonal favorites. In the summertime, foods taste better on a stick!

SAUTÉED SWISS CHARD AND
PINE NUT BRUSCHETTA

Sautéed Swiss Chard and Pine Nut Bruschetta

If you've never tried Swiss chard (a dark leafy green similar to kale and spinach), this pretty appetizer makes a good introduction. Garlic, red onion, currants, vinegar and honey balance its earthiness.

PREP 15 minutes **BAKE** 10 minutes **COOK** 17 minutes

- 1 pound fresh green or red Swiss chard or spinach
- 1 12-ounce loaf baguette-style French bread, sliced diagonally into ½-inch slices
- 4 tablespoons olive oil
- ⅓ cup chopped red onion
- ¼ teaspoon sea salt
- 2 tablespoons currants
- 2 cloves garlic, minced
- 1 tablespoon balsamic vinegar
- 1 teaspoon honey
  Sea salt
  Ground black pepper
- ¼ cup pine nuts, toasted (see tip, page 39)

1. Thoroughly wash Swiss chard or spinach by submerging it repeatedly in a large amount of cold water. Drain well. Discard any discolored leaves. Cut out the center ribs from Swiss chard. (If using spinach, remove stems.) Finely chop stems and leaves, keeping them separate from one another; set aside.

2. Arrange bread slices on a large baking sheet. Brush with 3 tablespoons of the olive oil. Bake in a 400° oven for 10 to 12 minutes or until toasted, turning slices once.

3. Meanwhile, in a very large nonstick skillet, cook and stir onion and ¼ teaspoon sea salt in remaining 1 tablespoon oil over medium heat about 10 minutes or until onion lightly caramelizes. Add the reserved stems, currants and garlic. Cook and stir about 5 minutes more or until stems are tender.

4. Gradually stir in the chopped leaves just until wilted. Remove from heat. Stir in vinegar and honey. Season to taste with salt and pepper.

5. Serve Swiss chard mixture on toasted bread slices; sprinkle with pine nuts.
Makes 24 servings.

Per bruschetta: 84 cal, 3 g fat, 0 mg chol, 181 mg sodium, 12 g carbo, 1 g fiber, 3 g pro.

Garden Sliders

For a no-cook starter, serve the squash in these sandwiches fresh rather than grilled.

START TO FINISH 30 minutes

- 1 15- to 16-ounce can Great Northern or cannellini (white kidney) beans, rinsed and drained
- 2 tablespoons olive oil
- 2 cloves garlic, minced
- ½ teaspoon Italian seasoning, crushed
  Salt
  Ground black pepper
- 1 medium yellow summer squash, cut into ¼-inch slices
- 1 12-ounce loaf baguette-style French bread, sliced diagonally into ½-inch slices
- 2 medium roma tomatoes, cut into ¼-inch slices
- 1 small cucumber, cut into ¼-inch slices
  Small celery top sprigs, small tomato wedges and/or pickle slices (optional)

1. For bean spread: In a blender or food processor, combine beans, 1 tablespoon of the oil, the garlic and Italian seasoning. Cover; blend or process until smooth. Season with salt and pepper.

2. To grill squash, toss squash slices with remaining 1 tablespoon olive oil. Place in a grill basket. Place basket directly over medium heat about 5 minutes or just until squash is tender, turning once.

3. Spread one side of each bread slice with bean spread. Top half of the bread with tomato, squash and cucumber slices. Top with remaining bread slices, spread sides down. Secure sliders with wooden toothpicks. If you like, top with celery sprigs, tomato wedges and/or pickle slices.
Makes 12 sliders.

Per slider: 120 cal, 2 g fat, 0 mg chol, 289 mg sodium, 23 g carbo, 3 g fiber, 6 g pro.

Tomato Galette

Tender Parmesan-pepper pastry folds over heirloom tomatoes, shallots, goat cheese and fresh herbs in a that's ideal for weekend brunch. Serve it warm or at room temperature, though the leftovers taste great cold—if you have any.

PREP 35 minutes   **CHILL** 30 minutes   **STAND** 40 minutes   **BAKE** 30 minutes

½ cup cold unsalted butter, cubed
1½ cups all-purpose flour
⅓ cup shredded Parmesan cheese
1 teaspoon cracked black pepper
4 to 6 tablespoons cold water
4 large heirloom tomatoes, cored (about 2 pounds)
1 teaspoon kosher salt
3 tablespoons fine dry bread crumbs
1 large shallot, very thinly sliced (½ cup)
2 teaspoons fresh thyme leaves
4 to 6 ounces aged goat cheese or feta cheese, crumbled
1 egg, lightly beaten
1 tablespoon water
2 to 3 tablespoons small leaves fresh basil

1. In a large bowl, cut butter into flour with a pastry blender until pieces are pea size.* Stir in Parmesan and pepper. Sprinkle 1 tablespoon of the cold water over part of the mixture; toss with a fork. Push moistened dough to the side of the bowl. Repeat, using 1 tablespoon of the water at a time, until all the dough is moistened. Form into a disk, wrap with plastic wrap and chill at least 30 minutes or up to 24 hours or until easy to handle.

2. Slice the tomatoes about ¼ inch thick and arrange on a wire rack over a pan, sink or paper towels. Sprinkle with salt and let stand for 30 minutes.

3. On a lightly floured surface, roll dough to a 13-inch circle (don't worry if it's not perfectly round). Fold in half and carefully transfer to a large baking sheet lined with parchment paper; unfold.

4. Spread bread crumbs evenly on pastry, leaving a 2-inch border. Layer tomatoes, shallot, thyme and goat cheese on bread crumbs. Fold crust over filling, pleating pastry as necessary and leaving filling exposed in center. In a small bowl, combine egg and 1 tablespoon water; brush on edges of pastry.

5. Bake in a 375° oven for 30 to 40 minutes or until crust is browned and crisp. Cool at least 10 minutes; serve warm or at room temperature. Sprinkle with fresh basil; cut into wedges. **Makes 8 servings.**

***Food processor method:** The first step can be done in the food processor. Place steel blade in food processor bowl; add flour and butter. Cover and process with on/off turns until pieces are pea-size. Add Parmesan and pepper; pulse just until combined. Transfer to bowl and proceed as directed.

Per serving: 300 cal, 18 g fat, 67 mg chol, 414 mg sodium, 26 g carbo, 3 g fiber, 9 g pro.

TEX-MEX

PICKLED ONIONS

TAPENADE

MEDITERRANEAN

ASIAN

Tomato Toppers

Mix up one of these toppers to spoon over summer-fresh, vine-ripened tomatoes.

Tapenade: Diced kalamata olives, chopped fresh oregano and basil, and olive oil.

Pickled Onions: Finely chopped red onion, red wine vinegar, fresh thyme, brown sugar, crushed red pepper and salt. Refrigerate for an hour or, even better, overnight.

Mediterranean: A dab of minced garlic, chopped fresh parsley and basil, lemon zest and salt.

Tex-Mex: A dab of minced garlic, chopped cilantro, lime zest, cracked black pepper and salt.

Asian: Minced fresh ginger, thinly sliced shallots or red onion, chopped cilantro, rice wine vinegar and salt.

Fruity Tomato Salsa

START TO FINISH 20 minutes

    3 yellow and/or red tomatoes, seeded and
        chopped
    1 cup chopped seedless watermelon
    1 mango, seeded, peeled and chopped
    ⅓ cup finely chopped red onion
    ¼ cup snipped fresh cilantro
    2 jalapeño chile peppers, halved, seeded
        and finely chopped (see tip, page 11)
    3 tablespoons lime juice
    2 teaspoons honey
        Kosher salt

In a medium bowl, combine tomatoes, watermelon, mango, red onion, cilantro, jalapeños, lime juice and honey. Stir gently to combine. Season to taste with salt. Cover and chill until ready to serve (up to 2 hours). **Makes 4 cups.**

Per ¼ cup: 20 cal, 0 g fat, 0 g chol, 32 mg sodium, 5 g carbo, 1 g fiber, 0 g pro.

FRUITY TOMATO SALSA

Any way you slice it, fresh salsa should be an exercise in simplicity. Feel free to switch the mango or melon for other summer fruits.

Whipped Fresh Herb Butter

Homemade butter is a great conversation starter; your friends won't believe you made it from scratch! Spread it on bread, rolls and toast or toss with hot steamed vegetables.

PREP 15 minutes

1 cup whipping cream
2 tablespoons assorted snipped fresh
   herbs (such as rosemary, oregano, basil,
   parsley and/or thyme)
¼ teaspoon sea salt

1. In a large mixing bowl, beat cream with an electric mixer (preferably a stand mixer with a wire whisk attachment) on low speed for 2 minutes or until the cream starts to thicken. Increase to medium to medium-high speed and beat for 6 to 8 minutes. The cream will first beat to stiff peaks, then butter clumps will form and a milky liquid will appear in bowl. Scrape down sides as needed.

2. When clumps form and no more liquid is released, transfer mixture to a fine-mesh wire sieve set over a mixing bowl. Using the back of a spoon, gently press out the excess liquid. Discard liquid.

3. Transfer butter to a bowl. Stir in herbs and salt. Store, covered, in the refrigerator for up to 5 days. **Makes ½ cup.**

Per tablespoon: 96 cal, 11 g fat, 29 mg chol, 71 mg sodium, 0 g carbo, 0 g fiber, 0 g pro.

Sparkling Lavender Lemonade

PREP 15 minutes **STAND** 10 minutes
COOL 1 hour **CHILL** 4 hours

2 cups water
1 cup honey
2 tablespoons fresh or dried lavender buds
1 cup lemon juice
2 cups sparkling water
   Lemon wedges or slices (optional)
   Sprigs of fresh lavender (optional)

1. In a medium saucepan, bring the 2 cups water, the honey and lavender buds just to boiling over medium heat; remove from heat. Let steep for 10 minutes. Pour through a fine-mesh sieve into a 2-quart pitcher; discard lavender buds. Let cool to room temperature; stir in lemon juice. Chill, covered, for at least 4 hours or up to 24 hours.

2. To serve, add the sparkling water to the lemon mixture. Pour lemonade over ice cubes in tall glasses. If you like, garnish with lemon wedges and/or lavender sprigs. **Makes 8 (6-ounce) servings.**

Per 6 ounces: 137 cal, 0 g fat, 0 g chol, 3 mg sodium, 38 g carbo, 0 g fiber, 0 g pro.

Lavender-Spiced Walnuts

PREP 15 minutes **BAKE** 20 minutes

   Nonstick cooking spray
4 teaspoons dried lavender buds
1 teaspoon dried rosemary
¾ cup sugar
1 teaspoon kosher salt or sea salt
½ teaspoon ground cinnamon
1 egg white
1 tablespoon water
4 cups walnut halves or pieces
   (about 1 pound)

1. Line a 15x10x1-inch baking pan with foil. Lightly coat foil with cooking spray; set pan aside.

2. In a spice grinder, coffee grinder or small food processor, combine lavender and rosemary. Cover; grind or process to a fine powder. In a small mixing bowl, combine lavender mixture, sugar, salt and cinnamon. Set aside.

3. In a large mixing bowl, beat egg white and the water on medium to high speed until stiff peaks form (tips stand straight). Add nuts; toss to coat. Sprinkle sugar mixture over nuts; toss to coat.

4. Spread nuts in prepared baking pan. Bake in a 325° oven for 10 minutes. Stir, separating any nuts that stick together. Bake for 10 minutes more. Transfer to a wire rack to cool. Break into pieces. Store in an airtight container for up to 2 weeks or freeze for longer storage. **Makes 7 (⅔ cup) servings.**

Per ⅔ cup: 462 cal, 37 g fat, 0 g chol, 292 mg sodium, 30 g carbo, 4 g fiber, 9 g pro.

LAVENDER-SPICED WALNUTS

Lemon Ricotta Pancakes and Blueberry Compote

Whole-milk ricotta makes these pancakes melt-in-your-mouth tender.

PREP 20 minutes **COOK** 20 minutes

½ cup granulated sugar
1 teaspoon cornstarch
2 cups fresh or frozen blueberries
¼ cup water
1 10-ounce jar lemon curd
1½ teaspoons orange juice
Pinch salt
1½ teaspoons butter
¼ teaspoon vanilla
2 cups all-purpose flour
2 tablespoons granulated sugar
2 teaspoons baking powder
½ teaspoon salt
1 teaspoon lemon zest
2 eggs, separated
1 cup whole-milk ricotta cheese
1½ cups whole milk
Powdered sugar

1. For compote: In a medium saucepan, combine the ½ cup granulated sugar and the cornstarch. Add blueberries, the water, 2 tablespoons of lemon curd, the orange juice and pinch salt. Bring to boiling, stirring constantly; reduce heat. Simmer, uncovered, over medium to medium-low heat until the blueberries are tender but not broken down and the mixture is slightly thickened, stirring occasionally. Remove from heat; stir in butter and vanilla. Set aside to cool slightly.

2. For pancakes: In a medium mixing bowl, combine flour, 2 tablespoons granulated sugar, the baking powder, ½ teaspoon salt and the lemon zest. In a large mixing bowl, combine egg yolks and ricotta cheese. Fold in flour mixture alternately with the milk. Set aside.

3. In a small mixing bowl, beat the egg whites on medium-high speed until stiff peaks form (tips stand straight). Gently fold egg whites into the cheese mixture.

4. Pour about ¼ cup batter onto a hot, lightly greased griddle or heavy skillet. Spread batter, if necessary. Cook over medium heat for 2 minutes on each side or until golden brown. Flip when surfaces are bubbly and edges are slightly dry.

5. To serve, stack three warm pancakes, spreading about a tablespoon of the remaining lemon curd between each pancake. Sprinkle with powdered sugar and spoon some of the blueberry compote over the pancake stack. **Makes 5 servings.**

Per serving: 672 cal, 15 g fat, 152 mg chol, 560 mg sodium, 121 g carbo, 8 g fiber, 16 g pro.

July is prime picking time at Midwest lavender farms. A collection of glass bottles displays a few varieties of the fragrant perennial. From left to right: 'Hidcote', 'Folgate', 'Coconut Ice', and 'Royal Purple'.

Very Cherry Hazelnut Coffee Cake

This tart cherry-studded cake is reminiscent of treats served on Grandmother's farm table.

PREP 35 minutes **RISE** 1 hour **BAKE** 18 minutes **COOL** 10 minutes

⅔ cup warm milk (105° to 115°)
1 package active dry yeast
⅓ cup unsalted butter, softened
½ cup sugar
2 eggs, separated
1 teaspoon lemon zest
½ teaspoon salt
2¼ cups all-purpose flour
½ cup cherry preserves
2 tablespoons unsalted butter
1 tablespoon fresh lemon juice
1 cup fresh or frozen unsweetened pitted
    tart red cherries, thawed and drained
¼ teaspoon ground ginger
¼ teaspoon ground cinnamon
3 tablespoons salted butter
½ cup chopped hazelnuts
    Powdered sugar (optional)

1. In a small bowl, combine milk and yeast. Let stand for 10 minutes.

2. In a large mixing bowl, beat ⅓ cup butter and ¼ cup of the sugar with an electric mixer on medium speed until smooth. Add egg yolks, lemon zest and salt; beat until smooth. Beat in yeast mixture. Beat in 2 cups of the flour just until combined.

3. Wash beaters. In a medium mixing bowl, beat egg whites until frothy; beat egg whites into dough. Spread dough evenly into a greased 15x10x1-inch baking pan. Cover and let rise in a warm place for 1 hour or until double in size.

4. In a small saucepan, combine cherry preserves, 2 tablespoons unsalted butter and the lemon juice. Stir over low heat until butter melts and mixture is smooth. Let cool. Scatter cherries evenly over dough; drizzle cooled preserve mixture evenly over cherries.

5. For crumb topping: In a small bowl, combine remaining ¼ cup flour and ¼ cup sugar, the ginger and cinnamon. Using a pastry blender or fork, cut in 3 tablespoons butter until pieces are pea size. Stir in nuts. Sprinkle crumb topping evenly over fruit topping.

6. Bake in a 350° oven for 18 to 23 minutes or until lightly browned. Cool in pan on a wire rack for 10 minutes. If you like, dust coffee cake with powdered sugar. **Makes 16 servings.**

Per serving: 226 cal, 11 g fat, 44 mg chol, 110 mg sodium, 29 g carbo, 1 g fiber, 4 g pro.

Minnesota's Brainerd Lakes region practically forces visitors to slow down. What you do at that pace will sound a lot like what families did a generation ago—such as casting a line off the dock at Gull Lake—and that's entirely the point.

Sweet and Spicy Steak Salad

Sirloin strips marinated in raspberry-chipotle vinaigrette get caramelized edges on the grill. Pile skewers on mixed greens with goat cheese and veggies, then pass the tongs and dressing.

PREP 30 minutes **MARINATE** 6 hours **STAND** 30 minutes **COOK** 4 minutes

1 pound boneless beef top sirloin steak, cut ¾ inch thick
¾ cup bottled raspberry vinaigrette salad dressing
¼ cup raspberry spreadable fruit
2 tablespoons snipped fresh cilantro
1 chipotle chile pepper in adobo sauce, drained and finely chopped (see tip, page 11)
1 4-ounce package goat cheese (chèvre)
6 cups baby arugula leaves, baby spinach leaves or mixed baby salad greens
4 roma tomatoes, cut into wedges
1 avocado, halved and sliced
2 cups sliced fresh mushrooms
  Fresh chives, snipped (optional)
  Freshly ground black pepper (optional)

1. If desired, partially freeze beef for easier slicing. Trim fat from meat. Thinly slice meat across the grain into bite-size strips. Place the meat in a resealable plastic bag set in shallow dish.

2. For marinade: In a small bowl, whisk together salad dressing, spreadable fruit, cilantro and chipotle pepper.

3. To marinate the meat, pour ½ cup of the marinade over the meat. Seal bag; turn to coat meat. Marinate in the refrigerator for 6 hours or overnight, turning bag occasionally. Chill remaining marinade until ready to use.

4. Meanwhile, shape the goat cheese into 12 balls. Cover and chill on a small plate until ready to use.

5. At least 30 minutes before grilling the meat, soak twelve 6-inch bamboo skewers in water.

6. Drain the meat; discard marinade. Thread meat in accordion fashion on the skewers, leaving ¼ inch space between each piece. Preheat a grill pan over medium heat. Grill steak 4 to 6 minutes or until meat reaches desired doneness, turning halfway through cooking time.

7. To serve, spread arugula on a platter. Arrange the cheese balls, tomato and avocado in separate piles over one half of the arugula. Arrange the mushrooms over the other half of the arugula. Place the meat skewers on top of the mushrooms. If you like, sprinkle with chives or black pepper. Whisk the remaining vinaigrette to combine; drizzle over salad or allow guests to pour their own. **Makes 4 servings.**

Per serving: 489 cal, 24 g fat, 112 mg chol, 390 mg sodium, 28 g carbo, 4 g fiber, 44 g pro.

Spicy Skirt Steak with Avocado Dipping Sauce

Skirt steak is a long, narrow cut of beef; you may have to order it from a butcher. If unavailable, use flank steak and cook over medium heat (not high) for 8 to 10 minutes.

PREP 30 minutes **STAND** 35 minutes **GRILL** 4 minutes

      1 English cucumber
      1 medium avocado, peeled and seeded
     ¼ cup sour cream
     ¼ cup roughly chopped fresh dill
      2 tablespoons lime juice
      2 teaspoons minced jalapeño pepper (see tip, page 11)
      1 teaspoon minced garlic
     ½ teaspoon kosher salt
      2 teaspoons kosher salt
      1 teaspoon dry mustard
      1 teaspoon chipotle chile powder
     ½ teaspoon ground black pepper
     ½ teaspoon ground coriander
     ½ teaspoon ground cumin
      2 pounds skirt steak, trimmed of excess fat
        Olive oil
        Cucumber Salad (recipe follows)

1. For dipping sauce: Cut about 3 inches from cucumber and coarsely chop (reserve remaining cucumber for Cucumber Salad). In a food processor or blender, place the cucumber, avocado, sour cream, dill, lime juice, jalapeño, garlic and ½ teaspoon salt. Cover and process or blend until smooth. Pour sauce into a bowl. Chill, covered, until ready to use.

2. For rub: In a small bowl, mix 2 teaspoons kosher salt, mustard, chipotle chile powder, black pepper, coriander and cumin; set aside. Cut steak into 12-inch-long pieces, if needed, to make them easier to handle on the grill. Lightly brush steaks on all sides with olive oil; season evenly with rub. Let stand at room temperature for 30 minutes.

3. Grill steaks on the rack of a covered gas or charcoal grill directly over high heat (about 500°) for 4 to 6 minutes for medium-rare, turning once or twice. Remove from grill; let stand for 5 minutes. Slice across the grain into ½-inch slices. Serve warm with avocado dipping sauce and Cucumber Salad. **Makes 6 Servings.**

Cucumber Salad: Slice the remaining cucumber. In a medium bowl, combine the sliced cucumber; 1 miniature yellow sweet pepper, sliced; 1 small shallot, sliced; ¼ cup chopped red sweet pepper; 2 tablespoons lime juice; 1 tablespoon olive oil; and 1 tablespoon chopped fresh dill. Season to taste with salt and ground black pepper.

Per serving: 363 cal, 22 g fat, 90 mg chol, 695 mg sodium, 7 g carbo, 2 g fiber, 33 g pro.

Steak Sandwich with Herbed Tomato Sauce

PREP 15 minutes **GRILL** 10 minutes
STAND 5 minutes

      2 tablespoons butter, softened
      2 tablespoons olive oil
      1 tablespoon snipped fresh oregano
      1 tablespoon snipped fresh rosemary
      2 cloves garlic, minced
      1 teaspoon smoked paprika
     ½ teaspoon salt
     ½ teaspoon cracked black pepper
      4 slices crusty artisanal bread, ½ inch thick
   1½ pounds 1-inch beef ribeye steaks
        Salt
        Ground black pepper
      3 cups assorted cherry tomatoes

1. In a small bowl, combine first eight ingredients (through cracked black pepper). Lightly brush cut sides of bread with some of the herb mixture. Set remaining herb mixture aside.

2. Season both sides of steaks with additional salt and ground black pepper. Grill on the rack of a covered gas or charcoal grill directly over medium heat for 10 to 12 minutes for medium rare (145°), turning once. During the last 2 to 3 minutes of grilling steaks, grill the bread until toasted. Set aside. Remove steaks, tent with foil and let stand about 5 minutes.

3. Meanwhile, heat a large skillet over medium-high heat. Add remaining herb mixture. When butter begins to bubble, add tomatoes. Cook and stir for 4 to 6 minutes or until skins split.

4. Thinly slice steak. Place one piece of bread each on four plates. Arrange steak slices on bread; top with tomatoes. **Makes 4 open-face sandwiches.**

Per sandwich: 492 cal, 32 g fat, 123 mg chol, 730 mg sodium, 19 g carbo, 3 g fiber, 35 g pro.

Grilled Pork with Cranberry Chutney

This recipe features Marina's Cranberry Chutney from Circle B Ranch in South Dakota. Buy it at circlebranch.com or substitute another chutney.

PREP 15 minutes **MARINATE** 4 hours **GRILL** 20 minutes **STAND** 5 minutes

1 12- to 16-ounce pork tenderloin
¼ cup olive oil
2 tablespoons cranberry or other
   fruit chutney
2 tablespoons dry white wine or lemon juice
2 tablespoons peach or apricot preserves
2 tablespoons reduced-sodium soy sauce
1 tablespoon Dijon-style mustard
1 teaspoon chopped fresh ginger
1 large clove garlic, minced
   Salt
   Freshly ground black pepper
   Cranberry or other fruit chutney (optional)

1. Trim fat from pork. Place meat in a resealable plastic bag. Set aside.

2. For marinade: In a small bowl, combine oil, 2 tablespoons chutney, the wine, preserves, soy sauce, mustard, ginger and garlic. With kitchen shears, snip any large fruit pieces. Pour marinade over meat. Seal bag; turn to coat meat. Marinate in the refrigerator for 4 to 8 hours, turning bag occasionally. Drain meat, discarding marinade.

3. For a charcoal grill: Arrange medium-hot coals around a drip pan. Test for medium heat above the pan. Place meat on the grill rack over the drip pan. Cover and grill for 20 to 30 minutes or until an instant-read thermometer inserted into meat registers 145°. (For a gas grill: Preheat grill. Reduce heat to medium. Adjust for indirect cooking. Place meat on a rack in a roasting pan; place on grill rack and grill as directed.)

4. Remove meat from grill; transfer to a serving platter. Cover meat loosely with foil and let stand for 5 minutes.

5. To serve, slice pork; season to taste with salt and pepper. If you like, serve with additional chutney. **Makes 4 servings.**

Per serving: 121 cal, 5 g fat, 52 mg chol, 233 mg sodium, 2 g carbo, 0 g fiber, 17 g pro.

One of the purest pleasures of summer is getting dirty in the garden, harvesting the best vegetables you've ever tasted.

Chimichurri-Stuffed Pork Loin

Fresh herbs, garlic and lime zest—in place of salt—flavor this pork loin.

PREP 40 minutes **GRILL** 1 hour **STAND** 10 minutes

1 cup loosely packed fresh Italian (flat-leaf) parsley leaves
1 cup loosely packed fresh cilantro leaves
1 tablespoon lime zest
3 tablespoons olive oil
3 large cloves garlic, minced
1 2½- to 3-pound boneless pork loin roast
¼ teaspoon ground black pepper
  Grilled Sweet Corn (recipe follows)
  Grilled Pineapple (recipe follows)

1. Snip 2 tablespoons each of the parsley and cilantro. In a small bowl, combine snipped herbs with ½ teaspoon of the lime zest, 1 tablespoon of the oil and one-third of the minced garlic; set aside.

2. Trim fat from pork. To butterfly pork, place meat on a cutting board with one end toward you Using a long sharp knife, make a lengthwise cut starting 1 inch from the right side of loin. Cut down to about 1 inch from the bottom of loin. Turn the knife and cut to your left, as if forming a right angle, stopping when you get to about 1 inch from the opposite side of the loin. Open roast to lie nearly flat. Brush with the remaining 2 tablespoons olive oil. Spread remaining minced garlic on surface. Sprinkle with pepper and remaining parsley, cilantro and lime zest. Roll pork to original shape. Tie at 2-inch intervals with 100%-cotton kitchen string. Spread snipped herb mixture on roast. Sprinkle with additional ground black pepper.

3. For charcoal grill: Arrange medium-hot coals around a drip pan. Test for medium heat above pan. Place pork on grill rack over pan. Cover and grill 1 to 1½ hours or until an instant-read thermometer inserted in center of pork registers 145°. Add more coals as needed to maintain medium heat above drip pan. (For a gas grill, preheat grill. Reduce heat to medium. Adjust for indirect cooking. Grill as directed.)

4. Remove pork from grill. Cover with foil; let stand 10 minutes. (Meat's temperature will rise after standing.) Remove string. Slice and serve with Grilled Sweet Corn and Grilled Pineapple. **Makes 4 to 6 servings plus leftovers.**

Grilled Sweet Corn: Brush 4 to 6 husked ears of corn with 2 tablespoons melted butter. Sprinkle with salt and ground black pepper. Grill directly over coals, turning occasionally during last 20 minutes of pork grilling time.

Grilled Pineapple: Grill 4 to 6 slices pineapple directly over coals, turning occasionally during the last 5 to 10 minutes of pork grilling time.

Per serving (with corn and pineapple): 385 cal, 15 g fat, 113 mg chol, 283 mg sodium, 30 g carbo, 4 g fiber, 35 g pro.

BBQ Pork Loin Ribs

Pork ribs do take a while—plan to light the grill 4 hours before you want to eat—but most of that time will be hands-off, so it's easy cooking. Ready? Let's get started!

PREP 40 minutes **STAND** 35 minutes **GRILL** 3 hours

- 4 to 5 pounds pork loin back ribs or pork spareribs
  All-Purpose BBQ Rub (recipe follows)
- ¼ cup honey
- ¼ cup beer, apple juice or pineapple juice
  Chipotle BBQ Sauce (recipe follows) (optional)
  Grilled Sweet Corn (see recipe, page 84) (optional)

1. Trim fat from ribs. If the bone side of the ribs looks smooth and shiny, the membrane is still intact. To remove membrane, insert a table knife under the membrane on one end to gently loosen it, then work your fingers under and peel it off in a sheet. To get a good grip, grasp it with a paper towel.

2. Sprinkle All-Purpose BBQ Rub over ribs; pat rub into meat. If you like, wrap ribs in plastic wrap and chill for up to 24 hours.

3. For a charcoal grill: Arrange medium-hot coals around a drip pan. Test for medium heat above the pan. (You can hold your hand 5 inches above where the food will cook for 6 to 7 seconds before having to pull away.) Place ribs, bone sides down, on a grill rack over the drip pan. Cover and grill for 2 hours, adding additional coals as needed to maintain temperature. (For a gas grill, preheat the grill. Reduce heat to medium. Adjust for indirect cooking by placing ribs in a roasting pan over unlit burner. Grill as directed.)

4. After 2 hours of grilling, tear off a piece of heavy foil large enough to enclose each slab; fold up edges a bit to create a rim. Drizzle the foil with honey and beer. Place ribs on foil and wrap; let stand at room temperature for 20 to 30 minutes. Return the wrapped ribs to grill; grill for 45 minutes more.

5. Remove ribs from grill. Unwrap ribs. If you like, brush ribs with Chipotle BBQ Sauce. Return the unwrapped ribs to the covered grill; grill for 10 minutes. Brush again with sauce; grill for 5 minutes more or until done.* Remove from grill and let the ribs stand at room temperature 15 minutes, loosely covered with foil. Cut the slabs into two- to four-rib pieces. If you like, serve ribs with Grilled Sweet Corn. **Makes 6 servings.**

***Tip:** To test doneness of ribs, twist two of the rib bones away from each other. The meat should easily pull away from the bones.

Oven Method: To bake ribs in oven, cut the seasoned ribs into more manageable pieces or leave as slabs. Place ribs, bone sides down, in a large, shallow roasting pan. (If the pan has deep sides, the meat won't cook efficiently.) Roast, uncovered, in a 325° oven for 1 hour. Baste ribs with Chipotle BBQ Sauce. Roast, uncovered, for 45 to 60 minutes more or until tender (meat will easily pull away from the bone), brushing once with additional sauce. Serve as directed.

Per ½ pound loin back ribs: 371 cal, 23 g fat, 97 mg chol, 466 mg sodium, 12 g carbo, 0 g fiber, 28 g pro.

All-Purpose BBQ Rub

START TO FINISH 10 minutes

- ¼ cup dried Italian seasoning
- 3 tablespoons paprika
- 2 tablespoons packed brown sugar
- 4 teaspoons ancho chili powder
- 2 teaspoons ground cumin
- 2 teaspoons celery salt
- 1½ teaspoons garlic-pepper seasoning

Combine all the ingredients in a clean jar with a lid. Store at room temperature for up to 2 months. **Makes ¾ cup.**

Chipotle BBQ Sauce

PREP 15 minutes **COOK** 25 minutes

- 1 small onion, finely chopped (½ cup)
- 3 cloves garlic, minced
- 1 tablespoon vegetable oil
- 1 cup ketchup
- ½ cup maple syrup or mild-flavor molasses
- ⅓ cup cider vinegar or lime juice
- 2 chipotle peppers in adobo sauce, finely chopped (see tip, page 11), plus 1 tablespoon adobo sauce
- 1 tablespoon Worcestershire sauce
- 1 tablespoon Dijon-style mustard
- ½ teaspoon salt

In a saucepan, cook onion and garlic in hot oil over medium heat until onion is tender. Stir in remaining ingredients. Bring to boiling; reduce heat. Simmer, uncovered, for 25 to 35 minutes or until slightly thickened and syrupy, stirring occasionally. Use sauce immediately. Or cool, cover and chill for up to 2 weeks. **Makes 16 servings.**

Stuffed Poblano Chiles with Sausage and Corn

When tough-skin chiles such as poblanos are to be used whole, they're best peeled.

PREP 45 minutes **ROAST** 20 minutes **COOK** 20 minutes **STAND** 15 minutes **BAKE** 10 minutes

8 fresh poblano peppers
1½ cups water
½ cup farro, rinsed
1 dried chipotle pepper
¼ teaspoon cayenne pepper
8 ounces sweet or hot Italian sausage
   (remove casings, if present)
½ cup finely chopped sweet onion
½ cup sliced celery
⅓ cup finely chopped green sweet pepper
1 fresh serrano pepper, sliced
   (see tip, page 11)
2 cloves garlic, minced
1 cup fresh corn kernels cut from the cob
¾ cup canned red kidney beans, rinsed
   and drained
¼ cup bottled diced pimiento or roasted red
   sweet pepper
1 teaspoon dried oregano, crushed
1 teaspoon chili powder
⅛ teaspoon cayenne pepper
   Sea salt
   Salsa (optional)

1. Place poblano peppers on a foil-lined baking sheet. Roast in a 425° oven for 20 to 25 minutes or until blackened and blistered. Place peppers in a bowl and cover with plastic wrap or place in a resealable plastic bag and seal. Let stand about 15 minutes or until cool enough to handle. Lift off skin, using a knife tip to loosen stubborn sections. Cut a slit in each pepper to make an opening; remove seeds and membranes. Set poblanos aside

2. For stuffing: In a small saucepan, combine the water, farro, chipotle pepper and cayenne pepper. Bring to boiling; reduce heat. Simmer, covered, about 20 minutes or until farro is tender; drain. Remove chipotle pepper from farro. If desired, remove stem and seeds from chipotle. Chop chipotle and stir into farro.

3. In a very large skillet, cook sausage for 5 minutes. Add onion, celery, sweet pepper, serrano pepper and garlic. Cook about 5 minutes or until vegetables are tender and sausage is no longer pink. Stir in farro, corn, beans, pimiento, oregano, chili powder and cayenne pepper. Heat through. Season to taste with salt.

4. Fill roasted peppers with farro-sausage mixture. Transfer to a shallow baking pan. Roast stuffed peppers in a 350° oven for 10 to 15 minutes or until heated through. If you like, top with salsa. **Makes 8 stuffed peppers.**

Per stuffed pepper: 181 cal, 3 g fat, 9 mg chol, 325 mg sodium, 28 g carbo, 4 g fiber, 11 g pro.

Children and chickens run wild between garden rows on a 1-acre urban farm in Springfield, Missouri.

MANGO-BARBECUE
FISH TACOS

Mango-Barbecue Fish Tacos

START TO FINISH 45 minutes

  1 mango, seeded, peeled and diced
½ cup barbecue sauce
¼ cup light mayonnaise
  1 teaspoon lime zest
  3 cups packaged coleslaw mix (shredded cabbage with carrot)
½ cup thinly sliced green onion (4)
12 ounces skinless red snapper, sea bass or cod, thawed, if frozen, and patted dry
  8 6-inch corn tortillas, wrapped in foil
½ cup purchased or homemade guacamole
½ cup chopped fresh cilantro
  Lime wedges (optional)

1. Place half the diced mango in a blender or food processor. Add barbecue sauce; blend or process until smooth.

2. In a large bowl, combine ⅔ cup of the barbecue sauce mixture, the mayonnaise and lime zest. (Set remaining barbecue sauce mixture aside.) Add remaining diced mango, the coleslaw mix and green onion. Toss to coat. Cover and chill.

3. For a charcoal or gas grill, grill fish on the greased rack of an uncovered grill directly over medium heat for 4 to 6 minutes per ½-inch thickness of fish or until fish flakes when tested with a fork, brushing generously with the reserved barbecue sauce mixture during the last 2 minutes of grilling. Place wrapped tortillas on grill rack over heat while fish is grilling, turning packet once.

4. To serve, use a fork to flake fish into bite-size pieces. Fill warm tortillas with fish, coleslaw, guacamole and cilantro. If you like, serve with lime wedges. **Makes 4 servings.**

Per 2 tacos: 344 cal, 11 g fat, 34 mg chol, 596 mg sodium, 41 g carbo, 5 g fiber, 21 g pro.

Pineapple-Chicken Stir-Fry

START TO FINISH 25 minutes

  4 teaspoons vegetable oil
  1 medium red onion, halved lengthwise and sliced
¾ cup zucchini cut into thin bite-size strips
¾ cup fresh pea pods, tips and strings removed
12 ounces skinless, boneless chicken breast halves, cut into thin bite-size strips
¼ of a fresh pineapple, peeled, cored and cut into bite-size pieces (1 cup)
  3 tablespoons bottled stir-fry sauce
  Brown rice (optional)
  Fresh pineapple wedges (optional)

1. In a wok or large skillet, heat 2 teaspoons of the oil over medium-high heat. Stir-fry onion in hot oil for 2 minutes. Add zucchini and pea pods. Stir-fry for 2 minutes more. Remove mixture from wok.

2. Add the remaining 2 teaspoons oil to hot wok. Add chicken. Stir-fry for 2 to 3 minutes or until chicken is tender and no longer pink. Return onion mixture to wok. Add pineapple and stir-fry sauce. Cook and stir about 1 minute or until heated through. If you like, serve over brown rice with pineapple wedges. **Makes 4 servings.**

Per serving: 188 cal, 7 g fat, 54 mg chol, 492 mg sodium, 12 g carbo, 1 g fiber, 19 g pro.

Guests at Grand View Lodge on Gull Lake In Nisswa, Minnesota, make s'mores over an open fire. Of the seven Gull Lakes in Minnesota, this Gull Lake is the largest. Anglers seek bass and walleye in its waters while pleasure seekers find treasure in the lodge's spa or one of several restaurants on the property.

Panzanella with Summer Vegetables

PREP 45 minutes **STAND** 30 minutes

4 ounces fresh green beans, trimmed and cut into 2-inch pieces
2 slices crusty country Italian bread, about 1 inch thick
1 tablespoon olive oil
2 large tomatoes, peeled,* if you like, and cut into 1-inch chunks
1 small cucumber, peeled, halved, seeded and sliced ½ inch thick
½ cup roasted red sweet peppers, cut into bite-size strips
½ of a small red onion, thinly sliced
¼ cup pitted kalamata olives, halved
¼ cup torn fresh basil leaves
¼ cup olive oil
2 tablespoons red wine vinegar
1 teaspoon Dijon-style mustard
1 clove garlic, minced
½ teaspoon sea salt
⅛ teaspoon cracked black pepper
Sea salt and cracked black pepper (optional)

1. In a large saucepan, cook beans in lightly salted boiling water for 2 minutes. Use a slotted spoon to transfer to a bowl of ice water to stop cooking. When chilled, drain and set aside.

2. Brush bread slices with 1 tablespoon oil. Toast on a grill or under the broiler until lightly browned, turning once. Cool slightly, then tear into 1-inch pieces.

3. In a large serving bowl, combine beans, bread, tomatoes, cucumber, sweet peppers, red onion, olives and basil.

4. For dressing: In a small screw-top jar, combine the ¼ cup olive oil, the vinegar, mustard, garlic, ½ teaspoon salt and ⅛ teaspoon pepper. Cover and shake well. Pour half of the dressing over tomato mixture; toss gently. Pour over remaining dressing. Cover and let stand for 30 minutes.

5. When ready to serve, toss again. If you like, sprinkle with additional salt and pepper. **Makes 6 servings.**

*To peel: Bring a large pot of water to boil over high heat. Meanwhile, core the tomatoes and make a small shallow X in the other end. When water comes to a boil, add tomatoes and cook for 10 to 15 seconds, until skin begins to loosen at the cuts. Using a slotted spoon, transfer to a bowl of ice water for 1 minute or until cool enough to handle. Remove skins.

Per serving: 175 cal, 13 g fat, 0 g chol, 304 mg sodium, 13 g carbo, 2 g fiber, 2 g pro.

ROASTED
JALAPEÑO
GAZPACHO

Roasted Jalapeño Gazpacho

Going to the trouble to roast a single pepper might seem unnecessary, but it adds a unique depth of flavor to the chilled soup.

PREP 30 minutes **ROAST** 20 minutes **STAND** 15 minutes **CHILL** 8 hours

  1 large jalapeño chile pepper
  1 teaspoon olive oil
  6 cups chopped, seeded tomato, assorted heirloom or red (6 large)
  2 cups chopped, seeded cucumber (about 2 medium)
  1 medium peach, peeled, pitted and chopped
  ¾ cup water
  2 tablespoons olive oil
  1 tablespoon red wine vinegar
  5 large fresh basil leaves
  1 large clove garlic, minced
    Sea salt
  2 tablespoons snipped fresh basil leaves

1. To roast jalapeño pepper: Halve lengthwise; remove stem, seeds and membranes (see tip, page 11). Place pepper halves, cut sides down, on a baking sheet lined with foil. Drizzle with the 1 teaspoon olive oil. Roast in a 400° oven for 20 to 25 minutes or until skins are blistered and dark. Carefully fold foil up to enclose pepper halves. Let stand about 15 minutes or until cool enough to handle. Loosen the edges of the skins from the pepper halves with a sharp knife; gently and slowly pull off the skin in strips. Finely chop skinned pepper halves; set aside.

2. Meanwhile, in a food processor or blender, combine 3 cups tomato, 1 cup cucumber and half of the chopped peach. Cover; process or blend until almost smooth but a few small pieces remain. Transfer tomato mixture to a large mixing bowl. In a food processor or blender, combine the water, 2 tablespoons olive oil, the vinegar, the five basil leaves and the garlic. Cover; process or blend until smooth. Transfer basil mixture to the bowl with tomato mixture.

3. Add the remaining tomato, cucumber and peach to the processed mixture, along with all or part of the roasted jalapeño pepper, to taste. Stir to combine; season with salt. Chill, covered, at least 8 hours or up to 24 hours.

4. Serve in small cups or bowls; garnish with snipped basil. **Makes 12 servings.**

Per ¾ cup: 48 cal, 3 g fat, 0 mg chol, 38 mg sodium, 5 g carbo, 1 g fiber, 1 g pro.

Roasted Carrots

Carrots' natural sweetness shines in this recipe, so shop your farmers market for the freshest ones, even if they aren't heirloom.

PREP 5 minutes **ROAST** 30 minutes

  1 pound medium heirloom carrots
  2 tablespoons butter, melted
    Sea or kosher salt
    Freshly ground black pepper

1. Trim tops from carrots. Scrub carrots; if you like, peel carrots. Dry well and cut any large carrots in half lengthwise.

2. In a 15x10x1-inch baking pan lined with foil, toss carrots with butter. Season with salt and pepper. Cover carrots with another piece of foil; roll edges of top and bottom foil together to make a packet.

3. Roast in a 425° oven for 15 minutes. Remove top foil sheet. Roast, uncovered, about 15 minutes more or until carrots are crisp-tender, stirring occasionally. Serve warm, seasoned with additional salt and pepper. **Makes 4 servings.**

Per serving: 98 cal, 6 g fat, 15 mg chol, 229 mg sodium, 11 g carbo, 3 g fiber, 1 g pro.

GREEN TOMATO
RELISH

Pickled Green Beans

Pickled beans are a farmhouse staple and common to old preserving books. They're great as part of a relish or antipasto tray and with burgers and brats at a picnic.

PREP 1 hour **PROCESS** 15 minutes

- 2 pounds fresh green beans
- 8 cloves garlic, peeled
- 8 small heads fresh dill*
- 2 small jalapeño peppers (optional)
- 2 teaspoons cayenne pepper
- 2½ cups water
- 2½ cups white wine vinegar or white vinegar
- ¼ cup pickling salt

1. Wash beans and remove ends and strings. In an uncovered 8-quart pot, cook whole beans in enough boiling water to cover for 5 minutes; drain.

2. Pack hot beans lengthwise into two hot, sterilized quart canning jars, leaving a ½-inch headspace. Add four cloves garlic, four heads dill, one jalapeño pepper (if using) and 1 teaspoon cayenne to each jar; set aside.

3. In a large stainless-steel, enamel or nonstick heavy saucepan, combine the 2½ cups water, the vinegar and pickling salt. Bring to boiling; stir to dissolve salt.

4. Immediately pour hot liquid over beans in jars, leaving a ½-inch headspace. Wipe jar rims; adjust lids.

5. Process filled jars in a boiling-water canner for 15 minutes (start timing when water returns to boiling). Remove jars from canner; cool on wire racks. Wait at least 5 days before serving. **Makes 16 (½-cup) servings.**

*Tip: If you cannot find fresh dill heads, use 3 tablespoons dill seeds.

Per ½ cup: 27 cal, O g fat, O mg chol, 447 mg sodium, 5 g carbo, 2 g fiber, 1 g pro.

Classic Succotash

Popular in the South, butter beans are a variety of fresh shelled beans similar to baby limas.

PREP 15 minutes **COOK** 35 minutes

- 2 cups fresh shelled butter or lima beans
  Kosher salt
- 2 large ears fresh corn (about 2 cups)
- 2 tablespoons unsalted butter
  Freshly ground black pepper
- ¼ cup heavy cream
- ¼ cup minced country ham

1. Place beans in a large saucepan. Cover with water; add about 1 teaspoon kosher salt. Bring to boiling. Skim surface until clear. Cook, partially covered, for 30 to 40 minutes or until tender. Strain beans into a large sieve; set aside.

2. Shuck corn. Using a clean terry-cloth kitchen towel, gently rub corn to remove silks. Using a sharp knife, cut corn kernels from cobs.

3. In a large skillet, heat butter over medium-high heat until melted and foaming. Add corn. Lightly season with salt and pepper, stirring to coat corn in butter. Cook 1 to 2 minutes. Add beans. Lightly season with salt and pepper. Cook 1 minute more, taking care not to overcook corn and beans.

4. Add cream and ham. Cook just until heated through and slightly reduced. Season to taste. **Makes 8 (½-cup) servings.**

Per ½ cup: 141 cal, 6 g fat, 2O mg chol, 246 mg sodium, 18 g carbo, 3 g fiber, 5 g pro.

Green Tomato Relish

This sweet-tart relish keeps well in the fridge, but if you like, it can be canned for longer storage or to be given as gifts.

PREP 25 minutes **COOK** 9 minutes
COOL 1 hour **CHILL** 2 hours

- 2 teaspoons mustard seeds
- ¼ teaspoon crushed red pepper
- ¾ cup sugar
- ¾ cup rice wine vinegar
- ¼ cup water
- 1 tablespoon grated fresh ginger
- 5 cloves garlic, thinly sliced
- 1 teaspoon salt
- 6 large green (unripe) tomatoes, cored and chopped (6 cups)
- 1 medium red sweet pepper, chopped
- 1 medium yellow sweet pepper, chopped
- 6 green onions, chopped

1. Cook mustard seeds and crushed red pepper in a hot Dutch oven over medium-high heat for 1 to 2 minutes or until seeds begin to pop. Add sugar, vinegar, the water, ginger, garlic and salt. Bring to a simmer; cook and stir for 3 minutes.

2. Add tomatoes and sweet peppers; cook for 5 to 7 minutes or just until vegetables are tender, stirring occasionally. Stir in green onions.

3. Transfer to a bowl or storage container. Cool for 1 hour. Chill, covered, for at least 2 hours or up to 1 week. **Makes 22 (¼-cup) servings.**

Canning: Prepare through Step 2. Ladle hot relish into six hot, sterilized half-pint canning jars, leaving a ½-inch headspace. Wipe jar rims and adjust lids. Process jars in a boiling-water canner for 10 minutes (start timing when water returns to boiling). Remove jars; cool on a wire rack.

Per ¼ cup: 22 cal, O g fat, O mg chol, 114 mg sodium, 4 g carbo, 1 g fiber, 1 g pro.

Tomato Pasta with Arugula and Parmesan

PREP 15 minutes **COOK** 15 minutes

10 ounces dried linguine pasta
5 cups assorted cherry tomatoes, halved
¼ cup olive oil
¼ cup snipped fresh chives
1 lemon, zested and juiced
4 cloves garlic, minced
½ teaspoon kosher salt
½ teaspoon cracked black pepper
4 cups baby arugula
2 ounces Parmigiano-Reggiano or Parmesan cheese, shaved or coarsely shredded (about ½ cup)

1. Cook linguine according to package directions. Meanwhile, in a medium bowl, combine tomatoes, olive oil, chives, lemon zest and juice, garlic, salt and pepper.

2. Drain pasta and return to pot over medium heat. Add tomato mixture and stir to combine. Heat through. Add arugula and stir just until wilted.

3. To serve, transfer to plates and top with shaved cheese. **Makes 5 servings.**

Per serving: 398 cal, 15 g fat, 8 mg chol, 407 mg sodium, 53 g carbo, 5 g fiber, 14 g pro.

Roasted Cherry Tomato Chutney on Spaghetti Squash

Toothsome strands of spaghetti squash stand in for pasta in this low-carb dish.

PREP 20 minutes **BAKE** 30 minutes

1 2-pound spaghetti squash, halved lengthwise and seeded
3 tablespoons olive oil
   Salt
   Ground black pepper
2 pints cherry and/or grape tomatoes
2 tablespoons minced garlic
¼ cup chicken broth
½ cup chopped onion
1 8-ounce container bite-size fresh mozzarella balls, cut up
¼ cup snipped fresh basil
2 tablespoons snipped fresh mint
   Freshly grated Parmesan cheese

1. Brush cut sides of squash with 1 tablespoon of the olive oil. Sprinkle with salt and pepper. Place squash halves, cut sides down, in a large baking dish. Prick all over with a fork. Bake, uncovered, in a 375° oven for 30 to 40 minutes, until tender.

2. Meanwhile, place tomatoes in a large bowl. Add the remaining 2 tablespoons olive oil, the minced garlic and salt to taste; stir to coat. Place tomato mixture in a 15x10x1-inch baking pan. Bake in oven with the squash the last 20 minutes.

3. In a large skillet, bring the chicken broth to boiling; add onion. Cook about 3 minutes or until tender. Remove skillet from heat. Add roasted tomatoes to skillet with the onion. Using a fork, gently press down on tomatoes to pop them. Add mozzarella, basil and mint to tomato mixture; toss well.

4. Using a fork, scrape the squash pulp from shell. Top squash with tomato mixture and Parmesan. **Makes 4 servings.**

Per serving: 360 cal, 24 g fat, 43 mg chol, 737 mg sodium, 22 g carbo, 5 g fiber, 14 g pro.

ROASTED CHERRY
TOMATO CHUTNEY ON
SPAGHETTI SQUASH

CHEDDAR TOMATO
COBBLER

Cheddar Tomato Cobbler

PREP 15 minutes **COOK** 15 minutes **BAKE** 35 minutes **COOL** 10 minutes

1 tablespoon olive oil
1 tablespoon cold butter
2 medium onions, halved and sliced about
    ⅛ inch thick
1 tablespoon packed brown sugar
¾ teaspoon sea salt or kosher salt
1 tablespoon balsamic vinegar
2 tablespoons snipped fresh oregano
6 cups cherry tomatoes
¾ cup all-purpose flour
¼ cup cornmeal
1¼ teaspoons baking powder
¼ teaspoon sea salt or kosher salt
¼ cup butter, cut up
¼ cup shredded cheddar cheese
½ cup milk

1. In a large oven-going skillet, heat oil and butter over medium-low heat. Add onions, brown sugar and ¾ teaspoon salt. Cover and cook for 10 to 15 minutes or until onions are very tender, stirring occasionally. Remove lid and turn heat to medium-high. Cook and stir for 5 to 10 minutes more or until onions are lightly browned. Remove from heat; add vinegar and oregano. Transfer mixture to a bowl or plate and set aside.

2. Place tomatoes in the skillet. Roast, uncovered, in a 400° oven about 15 minutes or until tomatoes pop and release their juices. Stir in reserved onion mixture.

3. Meanwhile, in a medium bowl, combine the flour, cornmeal, baking powder and ¼ teaspoon salt. Using a pastry blender, cut butter into flour mixture until pieces are pea size. Stir in cheese, then milk until all dough is moistened.

4. Remove skillet from oven. Carefully drop dough onto tomato mixture in eight mounds, spacing mounds evenly. Bake about 20 minutes more or until a wooden toothpick inserted into biscuits comes out clean. Cool on wire rack for 10 minutes. Serve warm. **Makes 8 servings.**

Per serving: 198 cal, 11 g fat, 24 mg chol, 406 mg sodium, 22 g carbo, 3 g fiber, 4 g pro.

Oven-Roasted Butternut and Beets with Arugula

This colorful blend is as nutritious as it is pretty. The veggies roast separately so the beets don't dye the squash pink.

PREP 20 minutes **ROAST** 25 minutes

2 pounds beets, peeled and cut into ½-inch
    pieces
¼ cup extra virgin olive oil
1 teaspoon salt
½ teaspoon freshly ground black pepper
1 2-pound butternut squash, peeled,
    seeded and cut into ½-inch pieces
2 cups baby arugula leaves

1. In a shallow roasting pan, combine beets, 2 tablespoons of the oil, ½ teaspoon salt and ¼ teaspoon pepper; toss to coat. In a second shallow roasting pan, combine squash, remaining oil, salt and pepper; toss to coat. Place roasting pans on separate oven racks and roast, uncovered, in a 425° oven for 25 to 35 minutes or until vegetables are tender, stirring and rearranging pans once.

2. Place beets and squash in a large bowl; add arugula and toss. Serve warm or at room temperature. **Makes 6 servings.**

Per cup: 76 cal, 4 g fat, 0 mg chol, 192 mg sodium, 11 g carbo, 3 g fiber, 1 g pro.

Potato-Thyme Frittata

PREP 15 minutes **COOK** 15 minutes **BAKE** 6 minutes **STAND** 10 minutes

  8 eggs
  ¼ cup milk
  1 tablespoon snipped fresh thyme or
      ½ to 1 teaspoon dried thyme, crushed
  ½ teaspoon sea salt or regular salt
  ¼ teaspoon freshly ground black pepper
  2 medium potatoes
  2 tablespoons butter
  ½ cup finely chopped onion (1 medium)
  2 cloves garlic, minced

1. In a medium mixing bowl, beat together the eggs, milk, thyme, ¼ teaspoon of the salt and the pepper. Set egg mixture aside.

2. Scrub potatoes and, if you like, peel. Rinse and dry well. Slice potatoes in half lengthwise. Cut each of the halves crosswise into thin, half-circle slices (should have 2 cups). Set potatoes aside.

3. In a large cast-iron skillet or ovenproof skillet, melt butter over medium heat. Add onion, garlic and the remaining ¼ teaspoon salt. Cook, uncovered, for 2 minutes, stirring occasionally. Add potatoes. Cook for 7 to 10 minutes or just until potatoes are tender and starting to brown, stirring occasionally. Before adding egg mixture, make sure vegetable mixture is spread evenly across the bottom of skillet.

4. Pour egg mixture over vegetable mixture in skillet. Cook over medium heat. As mixture sets, run a spatula around edge of skillet, lifting egg mixture so uncooked portion flows underneath. Continue cooking and lifting edges until egg mixture is almost set, about 6 to 8 minutes total (surface will be moist).

5. Place skillet in a 350° oven and bake, uncovered, for 6 to 8 minutes or just until top is set. (Or place skillet under a preheated broiler, 4 to 5 inches from heat. Broil for 1 to 2 minutes or until top is set.)

6. Let stand for 10 minutes before cutting into wedges. **Makes 6 servings.**

Per serving: 174 cal, 10 g fat, 259 mg chol, 325 mg sodium, 3 g carbo, 1 g fiber, 10 g pro.

Squash Ribbons with Parmesan and Crisp Prosciutto

A quality Parmesan will make a big difference in this simple recipe, which features just a few ingredients.

START TO FINISH 20 minutes

  2 medium zucchini
  2 medium yellow summer squash
  2 ounces very thinly sliced prosciutto
      (3 to 4 slices)
  2 tablespoons butter
  1 teaspoon cracked black pepper
  4 ounces Parmesan cheese, shaved into thin
      slices (curls) with a vegetable peeler

1. For squash ribbons: Trim each end of the zucchini and summer squash; rinse and pat dry with paper towels. Using a vegetable peeler, cut wide ribbons from the length of the zucchini and summer squash. (Slices should be slightly less than ⅛ inch thick.) Rotate the squash, peeling all four sides to get the most color; stop when you get to the seeds. Set aside ribbons; discard squash centers.

2. In a very large nonstick skillet, cook prosciutto over medium-high heat about 6 minutes or until crisp, turning once. Drain off and discard drippings. Crumble prosciutto and set aside.

3. In the same skillet, melt butter over medium heat. Add squash ribbons and cook about 2 minutes or just until tender, turning occasionally. Sprinkle with cracked pepper; remove skillet from heat. Add Parmesan cheese; toss gently and transfer to a serving platter. Top with crumbled prosciutto. **Makes 6 servings.**

Per serving: 148 cal, 10 g fat, 33 mg chol, 564 mg sodium, 4 g carbo, 1 g fiber, 11 g pro.

SQUASH RIBBONS
WITH PARMESAN
AND CRISP
PROSCIUTTO

You can still drive on the original brick portions of the Lincoln Highway when shopping the 1,200 garage sales that make up Ohio's Buy-Way each August. Small towns and a haunted prison dot the farm-flecked landscape.

Raspberry Angel Food Cake

From-scratch angel food is easier than you think, tastes better than store-bought and is one of the most healthy cakes around—no fat and just 178 calories per slice. Our version has a fruity swirl, but you can skip it if you like.

PREP 60 minutes **STAND** 30 minutes **BAKE** 40 minutes **COOL** 1 hour 30 minutes

1½ cups egg whites (10 to 12 large)
1½ cups sifted powdered sugar
1 cup sifted cake flour or sifted
    all-purpose flour
1 teaspoon cream of tartar
1 teaspoon vanilla
1 cup granulated sugar
¾ cup raspberries
    Raspberries and/or mango slices

1. In an extra-large mixing bowl, allow the egg whites to stand at room temperature for 30 minutes. Adjust baking rack to the lowest position in oven.

2. Meanwhile, in a medium mixing bowl, sift powdered sugar and flour together three times; set aside.

3. Add cream of tartar and vanilla to egg whites. Beat with an electric mixer on medium speed until soft peaks form (tips curl). Gradually add granulated sugar, about 2 tablespoons at a time, beating until stiff peaks form (tips stand straight).

4. Sift about one-fourth of the flour mixture over beaten egg whites; fold in gently using a large balloon wire whisk or a slotted skimmer. If using a whisk, periodically gently shake out the batter that collects on the inside. (If bowl is too full, transfer to a larger bowl.) Repeat, gently folding in remaining flour mixture by fourths.

5. In a small bowl, use a fork to crush the ¾ cup raspberries. Strain berries through a fine-mesh wire sieve to measure ¼ cup; discard seeds. Gently spoon one-third of the batter evenly into an ungreased 10-inch tube pan.* Spoon 2 tablespoons of the berries over the egg whites, keeping away from the edges. Spoon another one-third of the batter into the pan; repeat with the remaining 2 tablespoons of berries. Top with the remaining batter. Using a table knife, gently swirl the batter to marble and to remove air pockets.

6. Bake on the lowest rack in a 350° oven for 40 to 45 minutes or until top springs back when lightly touched. Immediately invert cake (leave in pan) onto the pan's legs (or over the neck of a metal funnel or tall bottle); cool thoroughly. Loosen cake from pan by sliding a narrow metal spatula or knife between the cake and pan in a continuous, not sawing, motion. Remove cake from pan and separate the cake from the pan bottom. Let stand for 1 hour. Serve at room temperature or lightly chilled. If you like, garnish with raspberries and/or sliced mango. Slice with a serrated knife. **Makes 12 servings.**

*Tip: Look for a straight-side tube pan with a removable bottom and metal "feet" for supporting the pan when you invert the cake to cool.

Per serving: 178 cal, 0 g fat, 0 mg chol, 51 mg sodium, 40 g carbo, 1 g fiber, 4 g pro.

Blackberry Clafouti

Cherries usually dot this French country dessert, but we opted for plump blackberries and a wisp of orange liqueur. Baked in a large skillet or a group of minis, the eggy batter yields a texture between cake and custard.

PREP 25 minutes **BAKE** 35 minutes

1 tablespoon butter, softened
3 eggs
½ cup granulated sugar
¾ cup whole milk
½ cup whipping cream
½ cup all-purpose flour
2 tablespoons orange-flavor liqueur or orange juice
2 teaspoons orange zest
1½ teaspoons vanilla
¼ teaspoon salt
3 cups fresh or frozen blackberries*
Powdered sugar
Crème fraîche or whipped cream

1. Brush a large cast-iron skillet, six mini cast-iron skillets or six 6- to 8-ounce ramekins with softened butter; set aside.

2. In a medium mixing bowl, beat eggs and granulated sugar with an electric mixer for 3 minutes or until light and lemon color. Stir in milk, whipping cream, flour, liqueur, orange zest, vanilla and salt.

3. Arrange berries in the prepared skillet. Carefully pour batter over berries. Bake in a 375° oven for 10 minutes. Reduce oven temperature to 350° and bake for 25 to 30 minutes more (20 to 25 minutes for smaller pans) or until filling is set and top is golden brown. Sprinkle with powdered sugar and serve warm with crème fraîche. **Makes 6 servings.**

*To use frozen berries: Arrange berries in a single layer on a baking sheet lined with paper towels. Let stand for 10 to 15 minutes (berries will not be fully thawed).

Per serving: 363 cal, 20 g fat, 155 mg chol, 178 mg sodium, 37 g carbo, 4 g fiber, 7 g pro.

An early-morning canoe ride is just one of many simple pleasures at historical Camp Wandawega in southeastern Wisconsin.

Mascarpone Flan Cake with Marinated Berries

This to-die-for cake comes from chef Debbie Gold at The American Restaurant in Kansas City, Missouri.

PREP 30 minutes   **CHILL** 1 hour plus overnight   **COOK** 15 minutes   **STAND** 10 minutes

2¼ cups pecans, toasted (see tip, page 39) and chopped (9 ounces)
1 cup walnuts, toasted (see tip, page 39) and chopped (4 ounces)
1 cup packed brown sugar
¾ cup butter, melted
1 envelope unflavored gelatin
¼ cup cold water
2 egg yolks
1 cup whipping cream
1¼ cups mascarpone cheese (10 ounces)
1⅓ cups powdered sugar
1 teaspoon vanilla
½ cup granulated sugar
1 cup dry white wine
1 cup blueberries
1 cup raspberries
1 cup strawberries

1. For crust: In a large bowl, combine pecans, walnuts and brown sugar. Stir in butter. Cut an 8-inch circle of parchment paper and place in the bottom of an 8-inch springform pan. Press nut mixture over bottom of pan. Chill for at least 1 hour.

2. For flan layer: In a small bowl, stir gelatin into the cold water; set aside to soften. Place egg yolks in a glass measuring cup; set aside. In a small saucepan, bring the whipping cream just to a simmer. Gradually whisk half the whipping cream into the egg yolks. Return egg mixture to the saucepan. Cook, stirring constantly, over medium heat until mixture reaches 145°. Remove from heat; set aside.

3. In a large mixing bowl, beat mascarpone with an electric mixer on low speed for 30 seconds or until smooth. Add powdered sugar. Beat until combined. Add vanilla and reserved egg yolk mixture. Beat until smooth.

4. In a small saucepan, cook and stir the softened gelatin over low heat until gelatin dissolves. Stir in ¼ cup of mascarpone mixture. Stir the gelatin mixture back into mascarpone mixture. Pour into the prepared crust. Cover and chill overnight.

5. For berries: In a small saucepan, combine granulated sugar and wine. Bring to boiling; reduce heat. Simmer, uncovered, about 10 minutes or until reduced by half.

6. Meanwhile, in a bowl, combine blueberries, raspberries and strawberries. Add ¼ cup of the berries to the wine mixture. Return to boiling; remove from heat. Let stand for 10 minutes; stir in the remaining berries. Cool completely.

7. To unmold cake, warm a thin knife in hot water and slide it around the edge of the cake's top layer. Remove the springform ring. Serve with the marinated berries. **Makes 14 servings.**

Per serving: 584 cal, 45 g fat, 102 mg chol, 113 mg sodium, 43 g carbo, 3 g fiber, 6 g pro.

Cherry-Berry Shortcake Stars

Tossing the cherries and blueberries with a little sugar draws out the juices. The sweet syrup is a perfect complement to the flaky, sconelike shortcakes. The dough for these shortcakes will be sticky. To easily cut out the star shapes, dip the cutter in flour between each cut.

PREP 20 minutes **BAKE** 12 minutes **COOL** 5 minutes

1½ cups fresh or frozen* tart red cherries, pitted
1½ cups fresh or frozen* blueberries
⅓ cup sugar
2 cups all-purpose flour
1½ teaspoons baking powder
¼ teaspoon salt
⅓ cup cold butter
1 egg
½ cup whipping cream
¼ cup honey
¼ cup fresh or frozen* tart red cherries, pitted and chopped
¼ cup fresh or frozen* blueberries, chopped
Vanilla Whipped Cream (recipe follows)

1. In a medium bowl, combine 1½ cups cherries, 1½ cups blueberries and the sugar. Set aside.

2. For shortcakes: In a large bowl, combine flour, baking powder and salt. Using a pastry blender, cut in butter until mixture resembles coarse crumbs. In a small bowl, combine egg, cream, honey, ¼ cup cherries and ¼ cup blueberries; add to flour mixture. Using a fork, gently stir mixture until moistened and dough comes together.

3. On a floured surface, knead dough by gently folding and pressing just until it holds together. Pat dough out to ¾-inch thickness. Using a floured 2½-inch star cutter, cut out shortcakes; reform scraps as necessary.

4. Place shortcakes 1 inch apart on an ungreased baking sheet. Bake in a 400° oven for 12 to 15 minutes or until golden. Cool on baking sheet for 5 minutes. Place two shortcakes in each of six serving bowls. Top with cherry-berry mixture and Vanilla Whipped Cream. **Makes 6 servings.**

Vanilla Whipped Cream: In a chilled medium mixing bowl, beat ½ cup whipping cream and 1 teaspoon vanilla with an electric mixer on medium speed until soft peaks form.

*Tip: If using frozen cherries and/or berries, thaw and drain well before using.

Per serving: 527 cal, 27 g fat, 113 mg chol, 339 mg sodium, 68 g carbo, 3 g fiber, 7 g pro.

Enjoy in-season blueberries in abundance—on shortcake, on your morning oatmeal, with yogurt and honey, or simply au naturel.

Peach-Topped Honey Rice Pudding with Chocolate

This recipes features a black raspberry dessert wine from Oovvda Winery in Springfield, Illinois, but any sweet wine will work.

PREP 15 minutes **COOK** 30 minutes

2¼ cups whole milk
 ½ cup uncooked long grain white rice
 ½ teaspoon sea salt
 2 tablespoons honey
 ½ teaspoon vanilla
 2 medium peaches, peeled, pitted and
    chopped
 ¼ cup Oovvda Black Raspberry Dessert Wine
    or sweet red wine
    Honey
 1 ounce 70% dark chocolate, chopped

1. For rice pudding: In a heavy large saucepan, bring milk to nearly boiling; stir in rice and salt. Simmer, covered, over low heat for 30 to 40 minutes or until most of the milk is absorbed, stirring occasionally to prevent sticking, especially near the end of the cooking. (Mixture may appear curdled.) Remove from heat. Stir in 2 tablespoons honey and the vanilla.

2. For peaches: Meanwhile, in a small saucepan, combine peaches and wine. Cook over medium heat about 15 minutes or until peaches are tender and wine is slightly reduced, stirring occasionally.

3. Serve warm rice pudding in bowls. Top with peaches, a drizzle of additional honey and a sprinkle of chocolate. **Makes 6 servings.**

Per serving: 214 cal, 5 g fat, 9 mg chol, 175 mg sodium, 37 g carbo, 1 g fiber, 5 g pro.

A seat in Indiana Dunes State Park on Lake Michigan is the perfect spot for watching the sunset.

Melon Sorbet

PREP 30 minutes **FREEZE** 11 hours **STAND** 5 minutes

1 cup sugar
1 cup water
⅓ cup light-color corn syrup
3 tablespoons lime juice
4½ cups seeded, cubed watermelon, cantaloupe or honeydew

1. In a heavy saucepan, cook and stir the sugar, water and corn syrup over medium-high heat about 5 minutes or until mixture comes to boiling. Remove from heat; stir in lime juice. Transfer syrup to a 2-cup glass measuring cup; set aside.

2. In a food processor or blender, puree half the melon for 30 to 45 seconds; add half of the syrup with machine running. Transfer to a flat 3-quart baking dish. Repeat with remaining melon and syrup.

3. For refrigerator freezer: Cover and freeze mixture for 5 to 6 hours or until almost firm, stirring once. Using a fork, break mixture into chunks. Transfer to a large, chilled bowl. Beat with an electric mixer on medium speed until smooth and fluffy but not melted. Return to the cold baking dish, spreading evenly. Freeze, covered, for 6 to 8 hours more or until firm.

4. For ice cream freezer: Chill covered mixture in refrigerator for 3 to 4 hours. Transfer mixture to a 1½ - or 2-quart ice cream freezer; proceed according to the manufacturer's instructions. Transfer sorbet to a freezer-safe, airtight container. Freeze for 3 to 4 hours to ripen, until firm.

5. Let sorbet stand for 5 to 10 minutes at room temperature before scooping. **Makes 10 (1-cup) servings.**

Berry Sorbet: In Step 1, substitute lemon juice for the lime juice. In Step 2, substitute 3½ cups raspberries, blackberries or chopped strawberries for the melon and add 3 tablespoons orange juice when pureeing the fruit. Press pureed fruit through a fine-mesh sieve into a bowl to remove seeds. Stir syrup into fruit, transfer to a 3-quart baking dish and continue as directed in Step 3 or 4.

Citrus Sorbet: Follow Step 1 as directed. In Step 2, substitute 2½ cups orange juice or 1 cup lemon or lime juice for the melon. Whisk the juice with the syrup, adding food coloring, if you like (no food processor or blender necessary). Transfer to a 2-quart baking dish and continue as directed in Step 3 or 4.

Per 1 cup: 133 cal, 0 g fat, 0 g chol, 8 mg sodium, 35 g carbo, 0 g fiber, 0 g protein

When the dog days hit, nothing—not even AC—beats cooling off with a scoop of sorbet. It's an instant antidote to summer's scorch—and so pretty, too! For a moment, you'll feel like a kid running through the sprinkler without a care in the world.

Fruit Hand Pies

Our flaky hand pies taste just like their big sibs, but they're tidier to serve and eat, making them perfect for potlucks and picnics. So what will it be—cherry, berry, peach or plum?

PREP 30 minutes **FREEZE** 30 minutes **CHILL** 45 minutes **BAKE** 16 minutes

½ cup butter, cut into ½-inch pats
½ cup shortening, cut into ½-inch pats
½ cup sour cream
2 egg yolks, lightly beaten
2 teaspoons lemon juice
2¾ cups all-purpose flour
2 tablespoons sugar
½ teaspoon salt
¼ teaspoon baking powder
1 egg, lightly beaten
1 tablespoon water
Fruit Filling, chilled (see recipe, right)
2 tablespoons coarse sugar

1. Place butter and shortening on a baking sheet lined with waxed paper; freeze 30 minutes. In a small bowl, combine sour cream, egg yolks and lemon juice; chill.

2. In a food processor fitted with the blade attachment, combine flour, sugar, salt and baking powder. Add butter and shortening. Pulse until butter bits are pea-size. Drop spoonfuls of the sour cream mixture over the flour mixture. Pulse until the pastry comes together but is still crumbly with visible butter bits. (Or cut in the butter and shortening with a pastry blender; stir in the sour cream mixture with a fork.)

3. Transfer dough to a large bowl and gently knead into a ball using floured hands. Divide dough into four portions; pat each into a 4-inch square and wrap in plastic wrap; chill 45 minutes or overnight.

4. When pastry has chilled, combine egg and the water in a small bowl for egg wash.

5. On a lightly floured surface or waxed paper, roll a dough portion to ⅛-inch thickness, leaving the rest in the refrigerator. Cut four circles using a 4-inch cookie cutter.

6. For round pies, place two pastry circles on a baking sheet lined with parchment paper. Spoon 2 heaping tablespoons of Fruit Filling onto center of each circle, leaving a ¾-inch border. Brush borders with egg wash. Prick remaining two circles a few times with a fork or cut a shape with a tiny cookie cutter. (We used a star.) Place pastry tops over filling; crimp edges with a fork to seal. For half-moon pies, place all four circles on the baking sheet. Spoon 1 heaping tablespoon of Fruit Filling on each circle. Brush border with egg wash, fold pastry, crimp to seal and prick twice.

7. Repeat with remaining dough to make a total of eight round or 16 half-moon pies. (If you like, reroll scraps to make a few more pies.) Brush pies with remaining egg wash; sprinkle with the coarse sugar.

8. Bake in a 375° oven for 16 to 18 minutes, until golden brown, rotating sheets once.
Makes 8 round or 16 half-moon pies.

Per round pie: 554 cal, 29 g fat, 106 mg chol, 282 mg sodium, 68 g carbo, 2 g fiber, 7 g pro.

Tip: Egg yolks and sour cream make our dough tender and pliable, but you can use refrigerated piecrust. You'll need two 15-ounce packages (four crusts). Let them stand at room temperature according to package directions to soften.

Fruit Filling

Choose one of the summer fruits below for your filling. Each recipe makes a bit more than enough for a full batch of hand pies. Spoon the extra over vanilla ice cream!

Cherry
3 cups pitted fresh or thawed frozen unsweetened tart cherries (with their juices)
1 cup sugar
2 tablespoons cornstarch
1 teaspoon orange zest
2 tablespoons orange juice

Blueberry
3½ cups blueberries
¾ cup sugar
¼ cup all-purpose flour
2 teaspoons lemon zest
1 tablespoon lemon juice

Peach or plum
3½ cups peeled, pitted and chopped peach or plum (1½ pounds)
½ cup sugar
3 tablespoons cornstarch
2 tablespoons butter
1 tablespoon lemon juice
⅛ teaspoon ground cloves

In a large saucepan, combine all the ingredients listed under the desired fruit filling. Cook over medium heat, stirring constantly, until thickened and bubbly. Set filling aside to cool. Chill, covered, about 2 hours.

LAVENDER
SHORTBREAD
COOKIES

Lavender Shortbread Cookies

PREP 30 minutes **BAKE** 13 minutes per batch

½ cup unsalted butter, softened
⅓ cup granulated sugar
¼ teaspoon salt
¼ teaspoon vanilla
1¼ cups all-purpose flour
1 to 2 teaspoons dried lavender buds, crushed
Coarse sugar (optional)

1. In a large mixing bowl, beat butter with an electric mixer on medium to high speed for 30 seconds. Add ⅓ cup sugar, the salt and vanilla. Beat until combined, scraping sides of bowl occasionally. Beat in flour (mixture will be more crumbly than typical cookie dough). Stir in lavender. Using your hands, form the dough into a ball and knead until smooth.

2. On a lightly floured surface, roll dough to about ⅜-inch thickness. Cut cookies using a 2- to 3-inch cookie cutter. (We used a flower.) Place 1 inch apart on ungreased cookie sheets. If desired, sprinkle cookies with coarse sugar before baking. Reroll dough as needed.

3. Bake in a 325° oven for 8 minutes. Rotate cookie sheet front to back. Bake for 5 to 6 minutes more or until edges are firm and lightly browned. Transfer cookies to a wire rack; cool completely.

4. Store cookies layered between waxed paper in an airtight container at room temperature for up to 3 days or freeze for up to 3 months. **Makes about 12 cookies.**

Per cookie: 141 cal, 8 g fat, 20 mg chol, 116 mg sodium, 17 g carbo, 0 g fiber, 1 g pro.

Pear-Plum Pie

PREP 40 minutes **BAKE** 1 hour 20 minutes

2 recipes Single-Crust Pie Pastry (see recipe, page 164) or 2 rolled refrigerated unbaked piecrusts
1¼ cups sugar
¼ cup cornstarch
1 teaspoon lemon zest
½ teaspoon ground cinnamon
Pinch salt
4 cups cored and coarsely chopped pear
2 cups chopped plum
1 small quince, cored, sliced and poached,* or 1 cup coarsely chopped pear
2 tablespoons lemon juice
2 tablespoons port (optional)
¼ teaspoon vanilla
1 egg, beaten
1 tablespoon whipping cream

1. Roll out one portion of pastry on a floured work surface to a circle about 12 inches in diameter. Transfer to a 9-inch pie plate without stretching. (Follow package directions if using refrigerated crust.) Trim pastry even with edge of pie plate.

2. In a small bowl, combine sugar, cornstarch, lemon zest, cinnamon and salt. In a large bowl, combine pear, plum and quince. Add lemon juice, port (if you like) and vanilla. Add sugar mixture; toss to coat. Transfer to prepared pie plate.

3. Roll remaining pastry portion into a 12-inch circle. Place on filling, gently molding over the fruit. Trim to ½ inch beyond edge of pie plate. Fold top pastry under bottom pastry. Crimp edge as desired. Cut four small slits in top crust to allow steam to escape. Combine egg and cream; brush on pastry. Place pie on a baking sheet lined with foil.

4. Bake in a 375° oven about 1 hour and 20 minutes, covering edge of crust with foil, if necessary, to prevent overbrowning. Cool on wire rack. **Makes 8 servings.**

*Tip: Simmer quince in boiling water for 5 minutes; drain.

Per serving: 491 cal, 23 g fat, 81 mg chol, 105 mg sodium, 68 g carbo, 4 g fiber, 5 g pro.

SLOW-COOKER BRAT
AND SAUERKRAUT
SOUP, PAGE 142

Fall

Harvest Fruit Butter

Use a variety of fruit and squash to make this delicious spread. Depending on the fruit used, there may be color and texture differences; however, flavor will be consistent if you adhere to spice and seasoning amounts.

PREP 25 minutes   **COOK** 1¼ hours

1 pound red or purple seedless grapes
1 cup 1-inch pieces peeled, seeded cooking-variety pumpkin and/or butternut squash
1 cup coarsely chopped fresh Mission figs (or ½ cup coarsely chopped dried Mission figs)
½ cup chopped pear or apple
½ cup raisins
½ cup water
1 tablespoon balsamic vinegar
1 teaspoon orange zest
½ teaspoon mustard seeds
½ teaspoon sugar
½ teaspoon salt
¼ teaspoon ground cloves
¼ teaspoon ground black pepper
Chopped toasted hazelnuts

1. In a Dutch oven, combine grapes, pumpkin, figs, pear and raisins. Add remaining ingredients, except nuts. Bring to boiling. Reduce heat.

2. Simmer, covered, for 30 minutes, stirring occasionally. Uncover; simmer for 45 minutes (30 minutes if using dried figs) over medium-low heat or until thickened and almost all liquid has evaporated. Cool completely. Transfer to a food processor. Cover and process until nearly smooth. Before serving, sprinkle with hazelnuts. To store, chill, covered, up to 1 week or freeze in tightly covered freezer containers up to 3 months. **Makes 2½ cups.**

Per 2 tablespoons: 40 cal, 0 g fat, 0 mg chol, 30 mg sodium, 10 g carbo, 1 g fiber, 0 g pro.

Spicy Chicken Wings

A meaty mix of wings and small drumsticks will satisfy the heartiest of appetites. Marinate and bake chicken ahead of time, then reheat on the grill for a hint of smoky flavor (or serve straight from the oven).

PREP 30 minutes   **MARINATE** 6 hours   **BAKE** 25 minutes   **GRILL** 10 minutes

1½ cups plain yogurt
2 tablespoons grated fresh ginger
3 cloves garlic, minced
2 teaspoons curry powder
1 teaspoon salt
1 teaspoon paprika
¾ teaspoon ground cinnamon
½ teaspoon cayenne pepper
4 pounds chicken wings and/or small chicken drumsticks
Fresh mint (optional)
Cucumber-Yogurt Sauce (recipe follows)

1. For the marinade: In a medium bowl, combine yogurt, ginger, garlic, curry powder, salt, paprika, cinnamon and cayenne; let stand for 15 minutes, stirring occasionally.

2. Meanwhile, if using chicken wings, cut each wing into two portions at the first joint. Place wings and/or drumsticks in a 2-gallon resealable plastic bag set in a shallow dish; add yogurt marinade. Seal bag and refrigerate for 6 to 24 hours, turning bag occasionally.

3. Drain chicken from marinade; discard marinade. Line two 15x10x1-inch baking pans with foil; lightly coat with nonstick cooking spray. Arrange chicken in prepared pans (if using both drumsticks and wings, place them in separate pans). Bake small drumsticks in a 400° oven for 35 minutes; bake chicken wings 25 minutes or until chicken is cooked through (180°).

4. Serve immediately, or cool chicken slightly and transfer to storage containers. Chill, covered, overnight and reheat.*

5. Transfer chicken to platter and, if you like, sprinkle with mint. Serve with Cucumber-Yogurt Sauce. **Makes 8 to 12 servings.**

Cucumber-Yogurt Sauce: In a bowl, combine two 6-ounce cartons plain yogurt; 1 large cucumber, shredded and well drained; 2 cloves garlic, minced; ½ teaspoon salt; ¼ teaspoon ground cumin; and 2 tablespoons chopped mint or basil. Chill, covered, and chill for 1 to 4 hours.

*Grill Reheat: For a charcoal or gas grill, place chicken on a well-greased grill rack directly over medium heat. Cover and grill 10 to 15 minutes or until heated through, turning once after 5 minutes. (Do not turn too soon or chicken may stick to grill. If chicken does stick, loosen with a metal spatula before turning.)

Per serving (with sauce): 343 cal, 21 g fat, 100 mg chol, 589 mg sodium, 10 g carbo, 1 g fiber, 28 g pro.

SPICY CHICKEN WINGS

BACON-CHEDDAR
CHEESE BALLS

Bacon-Cheddar Cheese Balls

Freshly shredded cheese works better than packaged shredded cheese in a cheese ball. Prepare the cheese mixture the night before so flavors have a chance to blend. Shape and roll in the crumbled bacon or pistachio nuts a few hours before serving.

PREP 40 minutes **STAND** 45 minutes
CHILL 2 hours

- 1 pound extra sharp cheddar cheese, finely shredded
- 2 8-ounce packages reduced-fat cream cheese (Neufchâtel)
- 1 2-ounce jar sliced pimientos, rinsed, drained, patted dry and chopped
- ¼ cup apricot preserves
- 2 tablespoons milk
- 1 teaspoon Worcestershire sauce
- ¼ teaspoon bottled hot pepper sauce
- 8 to 10 slices bacon, crisp-cooked and crumbled
- ⅓ cup pistachio nuts, chopped
  Celery stalks, cucumber slices, apricot halves and/or toasted baguette slices

1. In a very large mixing bowl, combine cheddar and cream cheese; let stand at room temperature about 45 minutes. Add pimientos, preserves, milk, Worcestershire, hot pepper sauce and about half the bacon (refrigerate remaining bacon). Beat with an electric mixer on medium speed until almost smooth.

2. Chill cheese mixture, covered, for 2 hours or up to overnight. Divide into two portions. On waxed paper, shape portions into balls. Up to 4 hours before serving, roll one cheese ball in bacon pieces and one in pistachio nuts. Serve with celery, cucumber, apricot and/or toasted baguette slices. **Makes 18 (¼-cup) servings.**

Per ¼ cup: 218 cal, 17 g fat, 49 mg chol, 361 mg sodium, 6 g carbo, 1 g fiber, 11 g pro.

Italian Meatballs

PREP 35 minutes **BAKE** 22 minutes

- Nonstick cooking spray
- 2 eggs, lightly beaten
- ½ cup seasoned Italian fine dry bread crumbs
- ⅓ cup grated Parmesan cheese
- 4 cloves garlic, minced
- ½ teaspoon salt
- ½ teaspoon ground black pepper
- 2 pounds lean ground turkey
- 8 ounces sweet Italian turkey sausage, removed from casings
- 2 tablespoons olive oil
- 1 teaspoon smoked paprika or paprika
- 1 cup Smoky Tomato Sauce (recipe, right)
  Small fresh basil leaves (optional)

1. Lightly coat a 15x10x1-inch baking pan with cooking spray; set aside.

2. In very large bowl, mix together eggs, bread crumbs, cheese, garlic, salt and pepper. Add turkey and sausage; mix well. With damp hands or an ice cream scoop, form twenty-four to thirty 1¾- to 2-inch meatballs (3 to 4 tablespoons each). Transfer to prepared baking sheet.

3. Combine oil and paprika; brush on meatballs. Bake meatballs in a 400° oven for 22 to 25 minutes or until cooked through (165° on an instant-read thermometer). With a slotted spoon, transfer meatballs to a large serving bowl; gently toss with 1 cup of the Smoky Tomato Sauce. If you like, top with basil. **Makes 12 to 15 servings.**

Per 2 meatballs with sauce: 180 cal, 7 g fat, 89 mg chol, 416 mg sodium, 6 g carbo, 1 g fiber, 24 g pro.

Smoky Tomato Sauce

Any leftover sauce is good served with sautéed chicken over pasta or as a dip for breadsticks. It can also be frozen for up to 6 months.

START TO FINISH 35 minutes

- 2 tablespoons olive oil
- 1 large onion, finely chopped
- 8 cloves garlic, minced
- 2 teaspoons dried basil or 2 tablespoons chopped fresh basil
- 2 teaspoons dried oregano or 2 tablespoons chopped fresh oregano
- 2 28-ounce cans crushed tomatoes, undrained
- ⅓ cup tomato paste
- 1½ teaspoons smoked paprika or paprika
- ½ teaspoon salt
- ½ teaspoon ground black pepper

1. In a Dutch oven, heat oil over medium-high heat. Add the onion, garlic, basil and oregano; cook, stirring occasionally, until onion is tender, about 4 to 5 minutes. Add the undrained tomatoes, tomato paste, smoked paprika, salt and pepper. Bring to boiling; reduce heat to medium-low. Simmer, covered, stirring occasionally, for 20 minutes.

2. Cool leftover sauce; transfer to a tightly covered container and store in refrigerator for up to 3 days or freeze for up to 3 months. **Makes 7 cups.**

Per ¼ cup: 34 cal, 1 g fat, 0 mg chol, 142 mg sodium, 6 g carbo, 1 g fiber, 1 g pro.

Feta, Honey and Date Spread

This spread can be made ahead and stored in the fridge up to 3 days. For a flavorful dipper, brush pita wedges with olive oil and sprinkle with salt and thyme before toasting in oven.

START TO FINISH 20 minutes

    1 cup crumbled feta (4 ounces)
    ½ cup toasted almonds, coarsely chopped
        (see tip, page 39)
    ½ cup pitted dates, chopped
    2 tablespoons fresh marjoram or
        1 tablespoon fresh thyme, chopped
    2 tablespoon coarsely chopped or sliced
        green olives
    2 teaspoons lemon zest
    ¼ cup honey
    ¼ teaspoon cayenne pepper
      Toasted pita bread wedges

In a serving bowl, gently stir together feta, almonds, dates, marjoram, olives and lemon zest. In a small microwave-safe bowl, combine honey and cayenne; warm in microwave 15 seconds. Drizzle over spread; fold gently to combine. Serve with pita bread. **Makes 12 (2-tablespoon) servings.**

Per 2 tablespoons: 168 cal, 7 g fat, 8 mg chol, 286 mg sodium, 24 g carbo, 2 g fiber, 4 g pro.

Simple diversions complement the apples and wine at Orchard Country Winery and Market in the Door County, Wisconsin, town of Fish Creek.

FALL VEGETABLE FAJITAS

Fall Vegetable Fajitas

Thinly slicing tougher cuts of meat, such as beef chuck eye steak, flank steak and skirt steak, ensures tenderness. To slice with ease, pop the steak in the freezer for about 20 minutes before slicing—it should be firm but not frozen. Hold a chef's knife at a 45-degree angle to the meat and thinly slice across the grain.

PREP 20 minutes **MARINATE** 2 hours **GRILL** 9 minutes

3 tablespoons chili-lime hot sauce
2 teaspoons vegetable oil
1 teaspoon dried marjoram, crushed
8 ounces boneless beef chuck eye steak, cut into very thin slices
1 medium zucchini, halved lengthwise and sliced
1 green sweet pepper, cut into strips
½ of a large red onion, sliced
6 8-inch flour tortillas
2 tablespoons snipped fresh cilantro
⅛ teaspoon ground black pepper
Sour cream, salsa and cilantro sprigs (optional)

1. In a large shallow dish, combine hot sauce, oil and marjoram. Add beef, zucchini, sweet pepper and red onion; toss to coat. Cover and refrigerate for 2 hours, tossing once; drain.

2. Preheat charcoal or gas grill to medium-high heat. Add meat and vegetables to grill basket. Grill, covered, for 8 to 10 minutes, stirring once, until meat is browned. Remove from grill. Place tortillas on grill grates; grill 1 minute, turning once.

3. Divide meat and vegetables among tortillas. Sprinkle with snipped cilantro and black pepper. If you like, top with sour cream, salsa and cilantro sprigs. Serve immediately. **Makes 6 fajitas.**

Per fajita: 254 cal, 11 g fat, 25 mg chol, 598 mg sodium, 27 g carbo, 1 g fiber, 12 g pro.

Peppered Steaks with Roasted Beets

START TO FINISH 30 minutes

2 pounds small golden and/or red beets with tops
1 tablespoon olive oil
⅛ teaspoon salt
⅛ teaspoon ground black pepper
1 pound boneless beef sirloin steak, 1 inch thick
¼ teaspoon salt
1 teaspoon cracked black pepper
Nonstick cooking spray
2 tablespoons water
1 tablespoon deli-style mustard
1 teaspoon packed brown sugar
½ of an 8-ounce package cream cheese, softened
½ teaspoon dried Italian seasoning, crushed

1. Trim and reserve beet greens; set aside. Peel beets; cut into wedges. Place in a 1½-quart microwave-safe dish. Cover with vented plastic wrap. Microwave on high 9 to 12 minutes or until tender, stirring once. Rinse and drain greens; tear to measure 1 cup. Drain beets. Add greens, olive oil, ⅛ teaspoon salt and ⅛ teaspoon ground black pepper to beets; toss to mix.

2. Meanwhile, season both sides of steak with ¼ teaspoon salt and 1 teaspoon cracked black pepper. Lightly coat grill pan or cast-iron skillet with cooking spray. Heat over medium-high heat. Cook steak 5 minutes per side or to desired doneness. For sauce: In a small saucepan, heat and stir the water, mustard and brown sugar over medium heat just until bubbly.

3. Cut steak into four portions and top with beets and sauce. Combine cream cheese and Italian seasoning; spoon over all. **Makes 4 servings.**

Per serving: 418 cal, 27 g fat, 83 mg chol, 418 mg sodium, 17 g carbo, 4 g fiber, 27 g pro.

Greek Burgers

PREP 20 minutes **COOK** 20 minutes

1½ pounds ground beef sirloin
2 teaspoons Worcestershire sauce
1 tablespoon snipped fresh oregano or
  1 teaspoon dried oregano, crushed
½ teaspoon kosher salt
¼ teaspoon freshly ground black pepper
2 tablespoons olive oil
1½ cups thickly sliced button mushrooms
2 small red onions, sliced
1 red sweet pepper, cut into strips
4 kaiser rolls, split and toasted
⅓ cup crumbled feta cheese

1. In a large bowl, gently mix the beef, Worcestershire sauce, half of the oregano, the salt and pepper. Shape into four ½-inch-thick patties. Set aside.

2. In a large cast-iron skillet, heat 1 tablespoon of the oil over medium-high heat. Add mushrooms, onions and sweet pepper. Cook and stir for 4 to 5 minutes, until crisp-tender. Transfer vegetables to a medium bowl; stir in remaining oregano and cover to keep warm.

3. Heat remaining oil in the same skillet over medium-high heat until very hot. Cook patties for 12 to 15 minutes or until an instant-read thermometer inserted in centers registers 160°, turning once. (If burgers brown too quickly, reduce heat.) Serve on toasted buns topped with vegetables and feta. **Makes 4 servings.**

Per serving: 652 cal, 37 g fat, 126 mg chol, 840 mg sodium, 37 g carbo, 3 g fiber, 41 g pro.

The prettiest stretch of Katy Trail State Park in Missouri passes near Rocheport. The trail offers 240 miles of easy, almost entirely flat pedaling.

GAME DAY CHILI

Game Day Chili

The Chili Seasoning Puree boosts the peppery flavor of the chili without being too spicy.

PREP 30 minutes **SLOW COOK** 6 to 7 hours (low) or 3 to 3½ hours (high)

Chili Seasoning Puree (recipe follows)
1½ pounds ground beef chuck
1 large onion, chopped
2 stalks celery, sliced
1 28-ounce can diced tomatoes, undrained
1 14.5-ounce can beef broth
1½ cups pitted dried plums, chopped
1½ cups water
1 6-ounce can tomato paste
2 tablespoons smoked paprika
2 teaspoons ground coriander
1 teaspoon crushed red pepper
¼ teaspoon ground cloves
1 ounce bittersweet chocolate, chopped

1. Prepare Chili Seasoning Puree. In a 6-quart Dutch oven, cook beef, onion and celery over medium-high heat, breaking up meat with a wooden spoon, until meat is browned and onion is tender. Drain off fat.

2. Transfer to a 5- to 6-quart slow cooker. Stir in Chili Seasoning Puree, undrained tomatoes, broth, plums, the water, tomato paste, paprika, coriander, crushed red pepper and cloves. Cook, covered, on low-heat setting for 6 to 7 hours (3 to 3½ hours on high-heat setting). Stir in chocolate and serve. **Makes 8 servings.**

Chili Seasoning Puree: In a small bowl, combine 2 dried ancho, mulato or pasilla chile peppers and enough boiling water to cover peppers. Let stand 30 minutes; drain well. Remove stems and seeds from peppers. In a food processor or blender, combine the drained chile peppers; ¾ cup beef broth; 5 pitted dried plums; and 1 fresh jalapeño chile pepper, seeded and chopped (see tip, page 11). Cover and process or blend until smooth.

Make-ahead directions: To make chili to store or tote, do not add chocolate. Cool slightly, transfer to a storage container and refrigerate up to 8 hours. Two hours before serving, return chili to slow cooker. Heat, covered, on high-heat setting for 1 to 2 hours, stirring occasionally. Stir in chocolate just before serving.

Per serving: 343 cal, 14 g fat, 58 mg chol, 702 mg sodium, 38 g carbo, 7 g fiber, 20 g pro.

Pork and Poblano Stew

This stew is low in fat, loaded with vitamin A and hearty enough to satisfy big appetites. The poblano pepper adds a punch of flavor so you don't miss the fat.

PREP 15 minutes **COOK** 24 minutes

1¼ pounds pork tenderloin, cut into ¾- to 1-inch pieces
2 teaspoons hot chili powder
2 tablespoons olive oil
1 fresh poblano chile pepper, seeded and cut into 1-inch pieces (see tip, page 11)
1 large red sweet pepper, seeded and cut into 1-inch pieces
1 medium onion, cut into thin wedges
1 14.5-ounce can fire-roasted tomatoes with garlic, undrained
1 14.5-ounce can reduced-sodium chicken broth
1 3-inch piece stick cinnamon
¼ cup fresh orange juice
2 teaspoons orange zest

1. Toss pork with chili powder to coat. In a large saucepan, heat 1 tablespoon oil over medium-high heat. Cook pork about 4 minutes or until browned, stirring occasionally. Use a slotted spoon to remove pieces; set aside.

2. Add remaining oil to the saucepan. Add poblano pepper, sweet pepper and onion; cook over medium-high heat until vegetables are just tender, about 5 minutes.

3. Add undrained tomatoes, broth and stick cinnamon. Bring to boiling; reduce heat. Simmer, covered, over medium-low heat for 10 minutes. Add pork and orange juice. Simmer, uncovered, for 5 minutes. Stir in orange zest. Remove stick cinnamon before serving. **Makes 4 servings.**

Per serving: 300 cal, 11 g fat, 87 mg chol, 534 mg sodium, 16 g carbo, 4 g fiber, 32 g pro.

Sweet Potato Salad with Ham

PREP 30 minutes **COOK** 10 minutes

2 pounds sweet potatoes, peeled and sliced
8 tender young carrots with tops, scrubbed or peeled and halved lengthwise
½ of a small red onion, sliced and separated into half rings
¼ cup olive oil
2 tablespoons white wine vinegar
1 tablespoon stone-ground Dijon-style mustard or Dijon-style mustard
⅛ teaspoon salt
⅛ teaspoon ground black pepper
1 teaspoon snipped fresh thyme
6 ounces ham, coarsely chopped
2 ounces blue cheese, crumbled
Fresh thyme sprig (optional)

1. Place sweet potatoes and carrots in a steamer basket. Cover and steam vegetables over simmering water for 10 minutes or until tender, adding the onion during the last 1 minute of steaming. Cool.

2. Meanwhile, for dressing: In a screw-top jar with a tight-fitting lid, combine olive oil, vinegar, mustard, salt and pepper. Replace the lid, then shake well to combine.

3. Place cooled potatoes, carrots and onion in a salad bowl. Gently fold in snipped fresh thyme. Top with ham and cheese. Drizzle with dressing; if you like, top with thyme sprig. **Makes 6 servings.**

Per serving: 278 cal, 13 g fat, 20 mg chol, 657 mg sodium, 31 g carbo, 6 g fiber, 10 g pro.

Pork Chops with Maple Apples

Cooking pork chops to the correct temperature ensures the best flavor, plus it confirms the meat is safe to eat. For an accurate temperature, insert a meat thermometer through the side of the chop into the center. Allowing the pork to rest while you prepare the apples gives it time to continue cooking. Don't skip this step!

PREP 15 minutes **COOK** 15 minutes
STAND 3 minutes

4 pork loin chops, cut ¾ inch thick
Salt and ground black pepper
1 tablespoon olive oil
2 cooking apples, cored and thinly sliced
1 small red onion, cut into thin wedges
2 cloves garlic, minced
¼ cup apple juice
⅓ cup whipping cream
1 tablespoon pure maple syrup
2 teaspoons snipped fresh thyme or 1 teaspoon dried thyme

1. Trim excess fat from pork chops. Sprinkle with salt and pepper. In a very large nonstick skillet heat oil over medium-high heat. Add pork chops. Cook for 8 to 12 minutes or until an instant-read thermometer registers 145°, turning once halfway through cooking. Remove from skillet. Cover with foil. Let stand 3 minutes.

2. Add apples, onion and garlic to skillet. Cook for 2 minutes, stirring occasionally. Add apple juice. Cook about 4 minutes more or until most liquid has evaporated and apples are crisp-tender.

3. Meanwhile, stir together cream, maple syrup and thyme. Pour over apples in skillet. Cook and stir 1 to 2 minutes or until heated through and sauce begins to thicken. Serve with pork chops. **Makes 4 servings.**

Per serving: 369 cal, 17 g fat, 108 mg chol, 234 mg sodium, 21 g carbo, 3 g fiber, 33 g pro.

Garlic Pork and Sweet Potato Hash

START TO FINISH 30 minutes

3 small sweet potatoes, scrubbed and chopped (4 cups)
1½ pounds pork tenderloin, cut into 1-inch slices
2 tablespoons reduced-sodium soy sauce
Ground black pepper
8 cloves garlic, peeled and thinly sliced
3 tablespoons vegetable oil
2 green onions, sliced
2 tablespoons honey
2 tablespoons water

1. In a large microwave-safe bowl, microwave potatoes, covered with vented plastic wrap, on 100% power (high) 8 minutes. Carefully remove plastic wrap; stir once.

2. Meanwhile, to butterfly pork slices, cut three-quarters through each; open and flatten slightly. Brush with some of the soy sauce and lightly sprinkle with pepper.

3. In a very large skillet, cook garlic in hot oil over medium-high heat just until it begins to turn golden brown. Remove and set aside. Cook pork in the same skillet 2 to 3 minutes on each side or until an instant-read thermometer inserted in slices registers 145°. Transfer to platter; cover. Add potatoes to skillet. Cook, stirring occasionally, until beginning to crisp. Add onions; cook 1 minute. Spoon onto individual plates; top with pork and garlic.

4. For sauce: In a hot skillet whisk together honey, the water and remaining soy sauce until bubbly. Drizzle over pork. **Makes 4 servings.**

Per serving: 450 cal, 16 g fat, 107 mg chol, 449 mg sodium, 39 g carbo, 4 g fiber, 37 g pro.

GARLIC PORK AND
SWEET POTATO HASH

Spinach and Sausage Skillet Pizza

PREP 35 minutes **COOK** 3 minutes **BAKE** 15 minutes **STAND** 5 minutes

1 15-ounce can tomato sauce
2 tablespoons tomato paste
3 tablespoons grated Parmesan cheese
¾ teaspoon dried oregano, crushed
½ teaspoon dried basil, crushed
⅛ teaspoon crushed red pepper
1 5- to 6-ounce package baby spinach
2 teaspoons water
   Olive oil
1 pound frozen pizza or bread dough, thawed
8 ounces bulk Italian sausage, cooked and drained
1½ to 2 cups shredded mozzarella cheese (6 to 8 ounces)

1. In a small bowl, whisk together the tomato sauce, tomato paste, 2 tablespoons of the Parmesan, the oregano, basil and crushed red pepper. Set aside.

2. Place spinach in a microwave-safe bowl. Sprinkle with the water. Cover with a microwave-safe plate and microwave on 100% power (high) for 30 seconds. Continue cooking in 10 second intervals until just wilted. Let stand for 2 minutes. Carefully remove plate. Transfer spinach to a sieve; press out liquid.

3. Brush a very large cast-iron or other heavy oven-going skillet with olive oil; set aside. On a lightly floured surface, roll dough to a 14-inch circle. Transfer to skillet. Roll edges to form a rim. Brush dough lightly with olive oil. Spread tomato sauce mixture over dough and top with sausage and spinach. Top with mozzarella and the remaining Parmesan.

4. Place skillet over medium-high heat for 3 minutes. Transfer to a 475° oven and bake for 15 to 20 minutes or until cheese and crust are lightly browned. Let stand 5 minutes. Using a spatula, slide pizza out of skillet to a large cutting board and cut into wedges. **Makes 6 servings.**

Per serving: 449 cal, 23 g fat, 53 mg chol, 1,237 mg sodium, 40 g carbo, 3 g fiber, 19 g pro.

Slow-Cooker Brat and Sauerkraut Soup

PREP 30 minutes **SLOW COOK** 6 to 7 hours (low) or 3 to 3½ hours (high)

1 pound uncooked bratwurst, cut into
    ½-inch-thick slices
1 pound tiny new red potatoes, quartered
2 small onions, cut into ¼-inch wedges or
    coarsely chopped
1 cup sliced celery
2 cloves garlic, minced
3 bay leaves
1 14.5-ounce can Bavarian-style sauerkraut
2 14.5-ounce cans lower-sodium beef broth
1 tablespoon spicy brown mustard
1 tablespoon cider vinegar
1 teaspoon paprika
1 teaspoon fennel seeds, crushed
½ teaspoon caraway seeds
    Sour cream (optional)

1. In a large skillet, cook bratwurst slices over medium-high heat for 3 to 4 minutes or until browned on all sides, stirring frequently. Remove from skillet; set aside.

2. In a 4- to 5-quart slow cooker, combine potatoes, onions, celery, garlic and bay leaves. Top with browned bratwurst and sauerkraut. In a large bowl, whisk together broth, mustard, vinegar, paprika, fennel seeds and caraway seeds. Pour into cooker.

3. Cover and cook on low-heat setting for 6 to 7 hours or on high-heat setting for 3 to 3½ hours. Discard the bay leaves. If you like, top each serving with sour cream. **Makes 6 servings.**

Per serving: 355 cal, 20 g fat, 55 mg chol, 1,335 mg sodium, 27 g carbo, 2 g fiber, 17 g pro.

Fall raking is a pleasure, not a chore, when the leaves are brilliantly colored and the air is refreshingly crisp.

Cajun-Rubbed Salmon

Fish made easy! Start with a quick sear—one of cast iron's best tricks—to seal in moisture; finish by baking in the oven. A simple pickle relish tops the spice-rubbed fish with tang.

PREP 25 minutes **COOK** 2 minutes **ROAST** 4 minutes

½ cup chopped celery
½ cup very thin strips red onion
2 tablespoons snipped fresh parsley
2 tablespoons chopped dill pickle
1 tablespoon pickle juice
1 tablespoon olive oil
2 teaspoons Dijon-style mustard
¼ teaspoon salt
　Dash sugar
4 6-ounce boneless salmon fillets
2 tablespoons Cajun Seasoning (recipe
　follows) or purchased Cajun seasoning
2 tablespoons olive oil

1. In a small bowl, combine first nine ingredients (through sugar). Cover and chill until ready to use or up to 1 hour.

2. Sprinkle salmon with Cajun Seasoning. Heat oil in a large cast-iron or other heavy oven-going skillet over medium-high heat. When hot, add salmon, skin sides up. Cook for 2 to 3 minutes or until lightly browned. Turn salmon. Place skillet in a 400° oven and roast for 4 to 6 minutes or until salmon flakes when tested with a fork. (Allow 4 to 6 minutes per ½-inch thickness of fish, including browning time.)

3. Stir onion mixture and serve with salmon. **Makes 4 servings.**

Cajun Seasoning: In a screw-top jar, combine 2 tablespoons packed brown sugar, 2 tablespoons paprika, 1 tablespoon kosher salt, 2 teaspoons dried oregano, 2 teaspoons dried thyme, 1 teaspoon garlic powder, 1 teaspoon ground cumin, ½ teaspoon crushed red pepper and ¼ teaspoon cayenne pepper.

Per serving: 356 cal, 21 g fat, 94 mg chol, 778 mg sodium, 5 g carbo, 1 g fiber, 34 g pro.

Cooking in cast iron gives you great results—it's a great conductor of heat—and can be healthy, too. Food absorbs traces of iron from the pan. Experiment with a pan to see what you like to cook in one.

Visitors to Warm Springs Ranch in Booneville, Missouri, can get up close and personal with the Anheuser-Busch Clydesdales and their foals. The 300-acre ranch is home to more than 100 of the stately animals.

Harvest Slaw

START TO FINISH 30 minutes

3 tablespoons olive oil
2 garlic cloves, coarsely chopped
2 teaspoons caraway seeds, lightly crushed
¼ cup cider vinegar
1 tablespoon honey
Salt
Ground black pepper
4 cups finely shredded red cabbage
2 red apples, cored and thinly sliced
½ cup dried cranberries
½ cup pecan halves, toasted (see tip, page 39)
2 tablespoons fresh cilantro or parsley leaves

1. In a large skillet, heat olive oil over medium heat. Add garlic and caraway seeds; cook and stir for 1 minute. Whisk in vinegar and honey; bring to a simmer. Season with salt and pepper.

2. In a large bowl, toss together the cabbage, apples, cranberries and pecans. Add dressing and toss to combine. Top with cilantro. **Makes 12 servings.**

Per serving: 108 cal, 7 g fat, 0 mg chol, 56 mg sodium, 13 g carbo, 2 g fiber, 1 g pro.

Roasted Cauliflower with Cranberries

Dress up cauliflower by roasting it with cranberries that almost burst as they cook. A sweet and tangy balsamic drizzle makes the dish a crowd-pleaser.

PREP 15 minutes **ROAST** 30 minutes

2 medium heads cauliflower (1½ to 2 pounds each), broken into florets
1 large yellow or red onion, cut into wedges
3 tablespoons olive oil
1 teaspoon kosher salt
1½ cups fresh or frozen cranberries
¼ cup balsamic vinegar
¼ cup honey
¼ teaspoon freshly cracked pepper
Mint leaves

1. Place cauliflower and onion in a baking pan. Drizzle with olive oil and sprinkle with ½ teaspoon of the salt. Stir to coat. Spread in an even layer.

2. Roast, uncovered, in a 450° oven about 30 minutes or until tender, stirring in cranberries halfway through cooking time.

3. Meanwhile, in a small saucepan, whisk together balsamic vinegar, honey, the remaining salt and pepper. Simmer, uncovered, until slightly thickened, about 10 minutes. Pour over cauliflower mixture; stir to coat. Transfer to a serving dish. Sprinkle with mint. **Makes 8 servings.**

Per serving: 135 cal, 5 g fat, 0 mg chol, 281 mg sodium, 21 g carbo, 4 g fiber, 3 g pro.

Bacon-Roasted Brussels Sprouts

PREP 15 minutes **ROAST** 20 minutes

2 slices bacon, thinly sliced crosswise
⅛ teaspoon crushed red pepper
2 pounds Brussels sprouts, trimmed and, if large, halved lengthwise
½ cup thin wedges red onion
2 teaspoons snipped fresh thyme
½ teaspoon salt

1. In a very large cast-iron or other heavy oven-going skillet, cook bacon over medium heat until browned and crisp. Remove bacon with a slotted spoon to paper towels. Add crushed red pepper to drippings in skillet; cook and stir for 1 minute or until fragrant.

2. Add Brussels sprouts, onion, thyme and salt to skillet. Stir to coat. Transfer to a 400° oven and roast, uncovered, for 20 to 25 minutes, stirring once or until just tender and browned. Sprinkle with reserved bacon. **Makes 8 servings.**

Per serving: 88 cal, 4 g fat, 6 mg chol, 234 mg sodium, 10 g carbo, 4 g fiber, 5 g pro.

BACON-ROASTED
BRUSSELS SPROUTS

SOUTHWEST
CORN PUDDING

Southwest Corn Pudding

PREP 25 minutes **BAKE** 30 minutes

1 tablespoon olive oil
1 tablespoon butter
1 medium onion, halved and thinly sliced
1½ cups fresh corn kernels (3 ears) or thawed frozen whole kernel corn
½ red sweet pepper, chopped (½ cup)
½ teaspoon ground cumin
¼ cup cornmeal
2 tablespoons all-purpose flour
½ teaspoon salt
1 14.5-ounce can cream-style corn
4 eggs, lightly beaten
1 4-ounce can diced green chiles, undrained
1 cup shredded sharp cheddar cheese (4 ounces)
1 tablespoon butter

1. In a large cast-iron or other heavy oven-going skillet, heat oil and 1 tablespoon butter over medium-high heat. When butter melts and bubbles, add onions. Cook, stirring occasionally, for 5 minutes. When onions are soft and starting to brown, add corn kernels, sweet pepper and cumin. Cook and stir for 3 minutes more. Set aside to cool slightly.

2. In a medium bowl, mix cornmeal, flour and salt; then gently stir in cream-style corn, eggs, undrained chiles and cheese. Fold onion mixture into cornmeal mixture. Set aside.

3. Return skillet to medium heat and add 1 tablespoon butter. When butter is melted, tilt skillet to coat bottom with butter. Pour batter into skillet.

4. Transfer skillet to a 350° oven and bake for 30 to 35 minutes or until a knife inserted near the center comes out clean. Serve warm. **Makes 10 servings.**

Per serving: 183 cal, 10 g fat, 92 mg chol, 389 mg sodium, 18 g carbo, 1 g fiber, 8 g pro.

Citrusy Mashed Squash with Toasted Pecans

PREP 15 minutes **COOK** 21 minutes

3 pounds butternut squash, peeled, seeded and cut into chunks
2 tablespoons butter
⅓ cup sour cream or ½ cup mascarpone cheese
¼ cup maple syrup
2 teaspoons orange zest
2 teaspoons lemon zest
¾ teaspoon salt
¼ teaspoon ground black pepper
2 tablespoons snipped fresh sage
½ cup pecan halves, toasted (see tip, page 39) and coarsely chopped
Sliced green onions and/or fresh sage leaves
Orange and lemon zest

1. In a 5- or 6-quart Dutch oven, cook squash in lightly salted boiling water, covered, 16 to 17 minutes or until tender when pierced with a fork. Drain.

2. Meanwhile, melt the butter in a heavy skillet over medium heat, whisking constantly until golden brown, 5 to 6 minutes. Transfer half the squash to a food processor. Add butter, sour cream, maple syrup, orange and lemon zest, salt and pepper. Cover and process until smooth. Place remaining squash in a bowl; add pureed mixture. Mash slightly. Stir in 2 tablespoons snipped sage.

3. Top with pecans, green onions and/or sage leaves and citrus zest. **Makes 8 to 10 servings.**

Per serving: 176 cal, 9 g fat, 12 mg chol, 258 mg sodium, 25 g carbo, 4 g fiber, 2 g pro.

Cumin-Rubbed Sweet Potatoes with Sage

The spiced butter makes enough for leftovers and is a zesty topper for pork or rice. To store, place the log in a freezer bag and freeze up to 6 months. Cut off slices as needed.

PREP 25 minutes **BAKE** 1 hour **COOL** 5 minutes

    4 medium sweet potatoes
    2 tablespoons coarse salt
    1 tablespoon cumin seeds, crushed
    ½ cup butter, softened
    1 tablespoon maple syrup or honey
    1 teaspoon crushed red pepper
      Canola or peanut oil for frying
      Fresh sage leaves

1. Wash and scrub potatoes. Mix together salt and cumin seeds. While skins are still damp, rub all over with salt mixture (reserve any remaining salt mixture for another use). Bake in a 375° oven directly on oven rack for 1 hour, turning once to crisp evenly on all sides.

2. Meanwhile, for spiced butter: In a bowl, stir together softened butter, maple syrup and crushed red pepper. Roll into a log using waxed paper; chill.

3. Heat 3 inches of oil in a medium saucepan over medium heat. Fry sage leaves 2 minutes or until crisp. Drain on paper towels.

4. Cool potatoes 5 minutes. If you like, brush off some of the salt from the skins. With a sharp knife, slice open lengthwise. Push the ends toward the center to open each potato. Top each with about 1 tablespoon of spiced butter and a few sage leaves. **Makes 4 servings.**

Per serving: 278 cal, 19 g fat, 31 mg chol, 527 mg sodium, 26 g carbo, 4 g fiber, 3 g pro.

Potato Latkes

PREP 10 minutes **COOK** 6 minutes per batch

    2 pounds russet potatoes
    1 medium onion, finely chopped (½ cup)
    ¼ cup all-purpose flour
    2 tablespoons snipped fresh parsley
    1 teaspoon salt
    ½ teaspoon ground black pepper
    ½ teaspoon baking soda
    2 eggs, lightly beaten
      Vegetable oil for frying
      Sour cream and/or applesauce (optional)

1. Peel and coarsely shred the potatoes; rinse in a colander. Place potatoes in three layers of 100%-cotton cheesecloth and twist to squeeze out moisture. Transfer to a large bowl.

2. Add onion, flour, parsley, salt, pepper and baking soda to potatoes and toss to coat. Add eggs and stir until combined.

3. In a large cast-iron or other heavy skillet, heat ¼ inch of oil. Drop heaping tablespoons of potato mixture into hot oil and flatten slightly. (Be careful not to crowd the pan.) Cook 3 to 4 minutes per side until golden brown, adjusting heat as necessary. Drain on paper towels. Keep warm on a wire rack set on a baking sheet in a 200° oven while frying remaining latkes. If you like, serve with sour cream and/or applesauce. **Makes 24 latkes.**

Per 2 latkes: 188 cal, 14 g fat, 31 mg chol, 262 mg sodium, 13 g carbo, 1 g fiber, 3 g pro.

POTATO LATKES

ONE-PAN
HARVEST PASTA

One-Pan Harvest Pasta

This comforting veggie-pasta dish is made for September, when fall is in the air but your garden hasn't gotten the memo.

PREP 20 minutes **COOK** 14 minutes

2 tablespoons vegetable oil
1 small eggplant, cut into 1-inch pieces
    (4 cups)
1 medium zucchini, coarsely chopped
    (2 cups)
2 tomatoes or 4 roma tomatoes, coarsely
    chopped (1 cup)
⅓ cup chopped red onion
2 cloves garlic, minced
1 19-ounce can cannellini beans (white
    kidney beans), rinsed and drained
1¾ cups reduced-sodium chicken broth
1 cup dried whole grain elbow macaroni
½ teaspoon crushed red pepper
    Salt
    Coarsely ground black pepper
    Snipped fresh basil
    Grated Parmesan cheese

1. In a very large skillet, heat oil over medium heat. Add eggplant, zucchini, tomatoes, red onion and garlic. Cook, uncovered, for 7 to 10 minutes or until vegetables are almost tender, stirring occasionally.

2. Add beans, broth, pasta and crushed red pepper. Bring to boiling; reduce heat. Simmer, covered, for 7 to 10 minutes more or until vegetables and pasta are tender, stirring occasionally. Remove from heat. Season with salt and pepper; serve topped with basil and Parmesan cheese.
Makes 4 servings.

Per serving: 357 cal, 10 g fat, 4 mg chol, 628 mg sodium, 52 g carbo, 14 g fiber, 16 g pro.

Caramelized Onion and Carrot Stuffing

The rich, deep sweetness of caramelized onions and roasted carrots epitomizes classic Thanksgiving flavors. A hint of tanginess comes from the sourdough bread.

PREP 30 minutes **COOK** 20 minutes
BAKE 45 minutes

¼ cup olive oil
2 large sweet onions, coarsely chopped
4 medium carrots, cut in chunks
    and/or sliced
⅓ cup butter
¼ cup torn fresh sage or 1 tablespoon dried
    sage, crushed
½ teaspoon kosher salt
½ teaspoon freshly ground black pepper
12 cups dry sourdough and/or wheat
    bread cubes
1 to 1½ cups chicken broth
    Fresh sage leaves (optional)

1. In a 4- to 5-quart Dutch oven, heat oil over medium-low heat. Add onions and carrots. Cook, covered, about 15 minutes or until vegetables are tender, stirring occasionally. Uncover; increase heat to medium-high and cook 5 to 8 minutes more or until onions are golden brown, stirring frequently. Remove from heat. Add butter. Stir until melted. Add sage, salt and pepper. Add bread; toss to combine. Drizzle with broth to moisten; toss lightly to combine.

2. Place stuffing in a 3-quart casserole. Bake, covered, in a 325° oven for 45 to 60 minutes or until heated through. If you like, top with fresh sage. **Makes 8 servings plus leftovers.**

Make-ahead directions: Prepare as directed through Step 1. Transfer stuffing to the casserole. Chill, covered, up to 24 hours. Bake, covered, 60 minutes.

Per ½ cup: 161 cal, 7 g fat, 11 mg chol, 306 mg sodium, 19 g carbo, 1 g fiber, 4 g pro.

Cheesy Butternut Squash Cavatappi Bake

This dish is packed with vitamin A and has less fat than traditional macaroni and cheese yet doesn't sacrifice taste.

PREP 30 minutes **COOK** 8 minutes **BAKE** 20 minutes

    Nonstick cooking spray
3 cups peeled and cubed butternut squash
2 tablespoons water
8 ounces dried cavatappi or other
    elbow macaroni
1 tablespoon butter
8 ounces cremini or button
    mushrooms, sliced
⅓ cup thinly sliced green onions (3)
2 tablespoons all-purpose flour
1 cup fat-free milk
¼ teaspoon salt
¼ teaspoon ground black pepper
1½ cups shredded Fontina cheese (6 ounces)
2 slices reduced-sodium bacon, cooked
    and crumbled (optional)
    Sliced green onions (optional)

1. Lightly coat a 2-quart rectangular baking dish with cooking spray; set aside.

2. In a medium microwave-safe bowl, combine squash and the water; cover with vented plastic wrap. Microwave on 100% power (high) for 4 minutes; stir. Microwave, covered, about 4 minutes more or until squash is tender. Carefully remove plastic wrap. Mash squash; set aside.

3. Meanwhile, cook pasta according to package directions; drain. In a medium saucepan, heat butter over medium-high heat. Add mushrooms and the ⅓ cup green onions. Cook until tender, about 5 minutes. Sprinkle flour over mushroom mixture. Cook and stir for 1 minute. Add milk, salt and pepper. Cook and stir over medium heat until thickened and bubbly. Remove from heat; stir in squash. Add pasta. Gently fold to combine.

4. Transfer half the pasta mixture to the prepared baking dish. Sprinkle with half the cheese. Add remaining pasta mixture and cheese. If you like, top with bacon. Bake, uncovered, in a 375° oven for 20 to 25 minutes or until heated through and cheese is melted. If you like, top with additional sliced green onions. **Makes 6 servings.**

Per serving: 334 cal, 12 g fat, 39 mg chol, 366 mg sodium, 42 g carbo, 3 g fiber, 16 g pro.

Whole Wheat Pretzel Rolls

Soft pretzels' chewy, brown exterior comes from being boiled in an alkaline solution—the ¼ cup baking soda in the water isn't a typo!

PREP 50 minutes **RISE** 2 hours **BAKE** 16 minutes **COOL** 10 minutes

2 to 2½ cups bread flour
1 package active dry yeast
1½ cups milk
3 tablespoons sugar
2 tablespoons vegetable oil
1 teaspoon salt
2 cups whole wheat flour
3 quarts (12 cups) water
¼ cup baking soda
1 egg white, lightly beaten
1 tablespoon water
Coarse salt

1. In a large bowl, stir together 1½ cups of the bread flour and the yeast; set aside. In a saucepan, heat and stir milk, sugar, oil and the 1 teaspoon salt just until warm (120° to 130°). Pour milk mixture into flour mixture and beat on medium speed for 30 seconds, scraping sides of bowl. Beat on high speed for 3 minutes. Stir in whole wheat flour and as much remaining bread flour as you can.

2. Turn dough out onto a lightly floured surface. Knead in enough of the remaining bread flour to make a moderately stiff dough that is smooth and elastic (6 to 8 minutes). Shape into a ball. Place in a lightly greased bowl, turning once. Cover and let rise in a warm place until doubled (about 1¼ hours).

3. Punch dough down; turn it out onto a lightly floured surface. Cover and let rest for 10 minutes. Shape into 12 smooth, oval rolls. Place them 2 inches apart on two greased baking sheets. With a knife or scissors, make a crisscross slash across each. Cover and let rise until nearly double (45 to 60 minutes).

4. Bake in a 475° oven for 4 minutes. Remove from oven. Reduce oven temperature to 350°.

5. In a large Dutch oven, bring the 3 quarts water to boiling. Gradually stir the baking soda into the boiling water (it will foam up slightly). Carefully lower rolls, two or three at a time, into the water and boil gently for 2 minutes, turning once. Remove with a slotted spoon and drain on paper towels for a few seconds before placing about 1 inch apart on baking sheets lined with parchment paper.

6. Whisk egg white and the 1 tablespoon water. Brush over rolls. Sprinkle with coarse salt.

7. Bake in a 350° oven for 12 to 15 minutes or until golden brown, rotating sheets halfway through baking. Immediately remove from sheets; cool on wire racks for 10 minutes before serving. **Makes 12 rolls.**

Per roll: 181 cal, 2 g fat, 2 mg chol, 724 mg sodium, 36 g carbo, 3 g fiber, 7 g pro.

Banana Bread

Make banana bread when your bananas get brown polka dots on them.

PREP 25 minutes **BAKE** 55 minutes
STAND overnight

2 cups all-purpose flour
1½ teaspoons baking powder
½ teaspoon baking soda
½ teaspoon ground cinnamon
¼ teaspoon salt
¼ teaspoon ground nutmeg
⅛ teaspoon ground ginger
2 eggs, lightly beaten
1½ cups mashed bananas (4 to 5 medium)
1 cup sugar
½ cup vegetable oil or melted butter
¼ cup chopped walnuts

1. Grease bottom and ½ inch up the sides of a 9x5x3-inch loaf pan; set aside. In a large bowl, combine flour, baking powder, baking soda, cinnamon, salt, nutmeg and ginger. Make a well in center of flour mixture; set aside.

2. In a medium bowl, combine eggs, mashed bananas, sugar and oil. Add egg mixture all at once to flour mixture. Stir just until moistened (batter should be lumpy). Fold in walnuts. Spoon batter into prepared pan.

3. Bake in a 350° oven for 55 to 60 minutes or until a wooden pick inserted near center comes out clean (if necessary, cover loosely with foil the last 15 minutes to prevent overbrowning). Cool in pan on a wire rack for 10 minutes. Remove from pan. Cool completely on rack. Wrap and store overnight before slicing. **Makes 1 loaf (16 slices).**

Per slice: 213 cal, 9 g fat, 26 mg chol, 108 mg sodium, 32 g carbo, 1 g fiber, 3 g pro.

BANANA BREAD

Cake Doughnuts

To avoid splashing hot oil and burning your fingers, lower doughnuts into the pan with a large slotted metal spoon.

PREP 30 minutes **CHILL** 2 hours **COOK** 2 minutes per batch

3½ cups all-purpose flour
1 tablespoon baking powder
1 teaspoon ground cinnamon
¾ teaspoon salt
½ teaspoon ground nutmeg
⅓ cup milk
½ cup butter, melted
4 eggs, beaten
⅔ cup sugar
Vegetable oil for deep-fat frying
Cinnamon-Sugar (recipe follows) or sifted
powdered sugar

1. In a medium bowl, combine flour, baking powder, cinnamon, salt and nutmeg; set aside. In a small bowl, combine milk and melted butter; set aside. In a large mixing bowl, combine eggs and sugar; beat with an electric mixer until thick, about 5 minutes. Add milk mixture to egg mixture; stir with wooden spoon to combine. Add flour mixture; stir with the wooden spoon until smooth. Cover dough; chill for 2 hours (dough will remain slightly sticky).

2. Turn dough out onto a lightly floured surface. Roll dough to ½-inch thickness. Cut dough with a floured 2½-inch round cutter. Use a 1½-inch cutter to cut the hole for the doughnut. (You can also use a standard doughnut cutter.)

3. Fry two or three doughnuts at a time in deep hot fat (375°) for 2 to 2½ minutes or until brown, turning halfway through with a slotted spoon. Drain on paper towels. Repeat with remaining doughnuts and doughnut holes.

4. Shake warm doughnuts in a bag with Cinnamon-Sugar or powdered sugar. Serve warm (or reheat each doughnut 8 to 10 seconds in microwave on high). **Makes about 15 doughnuts and doughnut holes.**

Cinnamon-Sugar: Stir together ½ cup granulated sugar and 1 teaspoon ground cinnamon.

Per doughnut: 382 cal, 20 g fat, 290 mg chol, 326 mg sodium, 39 g carbo, 1 g fiber, 11 g pro.

A toss with powdered sugar or Cinnamon-Sugar while they are still warm is the crowning touch onto these delicious doughnuts. They're fun to make with kids on a leisurely Saturday morning.

A stunning display of fall foliage contrasts beautifully with the brilliant blue water of Sturgeon Bay, at the southern end of Wisconsin's Door County peninsula. The town of Sturgeon Bay is rife with galleries, shops and restaurants—including those that feature the classic Door County fish boil.

Fall Fruit Cobbler with Cinnamon Ice Cream

No rolling or cutting necessary. Just pinch off portions of dough and pat them into rounds before laying them on the fruit filling.

PREP 20 minutes **BAKE** 35 minutes **COOL** 30 minutes

1½ cups cranberries
½ cup dried red cherries
½ cup water
⅔ cup granulated sugar
3 tablespoons all-purpose flour
2 pounds large plums, pitted and cut into chunks
1½ cups all-purpose flour
½ cup regular or quick-cooking rolled oats
2 tablespoons packed brown sugar
1½ teaspoons baking powder
½ teaspoon salt
½ teaspoon cream of tartar
6 tablespoons cold butter
½ cup milk, plus additional for brushing
Brown sugar
Purchased cinnamon ice cream

1. In a large cast-iron or other oven-going skillet, combine cranberries, cherries and the water. Stir in the granulated sugar and the 3 tablespoons flour. Cook and stir over medium heat until hot and bubbly. Stir in plums. Set aside.

2. In a large bowl, combine the 1½ cups flour, the oats, 2 tablespoons brown sugar, baking powder, salt and cream of tartar. Using a pastry blender, cut in butter until mixture resembles coarse crumbs. Make a well in center of flour mixture. Add milk all at once. Using a fork, stir just until moistened. Gently fold and press dough against the side of the bowl with your hands until it comes together.

3. Lightly flatten small portions of dough with your hands; place on filling in skillet. Brush dough lightly with milk; sprinkle with additional brown sugar.

4. Bake in a 375° oven for 35 to 40 minutes or until topping is golden brown and filling is bubbly. (If necessary, cover with foil during last 10 minutes to prevent overbrowning.) Cool for 30 minutes before serving. Serve with cinnamon ice cream. **Makes 8 servings.**

For a 9-inch deep-dish pie plate: Prepare filling in a large saucepan; transfer to pie plate. Continue as directed in Step 2.

Per serving: 526 cal, 19 g fat, 73 mg chol, 358 mg sodium, 85 g carbo, 5 g fiber, 8 g pro.

When the leaves turn and the air gets nippy, it's time to pack the cooler and have some good old-fashioned outdoor fun before winter. A pumpkin-patch picnic is the perfect activity.

Maple Pumpkin Pie with Salted Pecan Brittle

Not-too-sweet maple in this velvety pie is just enough tweak to make a second slice hard to resist. Prepare the sparkling pecan brittle up to a week ahead, then sprinkle on just before serving.

PREP 45 minutes **BAKE** 55 minutes **CHILL** 2 hours

Single-Crust Pie Pastry (recipe follows)
1 15-ounce can pumpkin puree
⅔ cup pure maple syrup
¼ cup packed brown sugar
1 teaspoon vanilla bean paste or
   vanilla extract
½ teaspoon salt
3 eggs, slightly beaten
¾ cup milk
Salted Pecan Brittle (recipe follows)

1. Prepare Single-Crust Pie Pastry; set aside.

2. For filling: In a large bowl, combine pumpkin, maple syrup, brown sugar, vanilla and salt. Add eggs; beat lightly with a fork until combined. Gradually add milk. Stir to combine.

3. Carefully pour filling in pastry shell. To prevent overbrowning, cover edge of pie with foil. Bake at 375° for 30 minutes. Remove foil. Bake for 25 to 30 minutes more or until a knife inserted near center comes out clean. Cool on wire rack. Cover and chill 2 hours. To serve, top with Salted Pecan Brittle. **Makes 10 servings.**

Single-Crust Pie Pastry: Stir together 1½ cups flour and ¼ teaspoon salt. Using a pastry blender, cut in ¼ cup shortening and ¼ cup butter until pieces are pea-size. Sprinkle 1 tablespoon cold water over part of the mixture; gently toss with a fork. Push moistened dough to the side of the bowl. Repeat moistening dough, using 1 tablespoon of the water at a time, until all the dough is moistened (¼ to ⅓ cup total). Form dough into a ball. Using your hands, slightly flatten pastry on a lightly floured surface. Roll pastry from center to edges into a circle about 12 inches in diameter. Wrap pastry around rolling pin; unroll into a 9-inch pie plate, easing it in without stretching. Trim pastry to ½ inch beyond edge of pie plate. Fold extra pastry under. Crimp as desired.

Salted Pecan Brittle: Line a baking pan with foil and coat with nonstick cooking spray; set aside. In a small saucepan, combine ¾ cup sugar and ¼ cup water. Stir over medium heat until sugar is dissolved. Bring to boiling. Boil, without stirring, until mixture turns a dark amber color, about 10 minutes. Stir in ¾ cup toasted chopped pecans and ½ teaspoon sea salt. Remove from heat; immediately pour onto prepared baking pan, spreading evenly. Immediately sprinkle with ½ teaspoon sea salt. Cool completely. Break into pieces. Store in a covered container at room temperature up to 1 week.

Per serving: 560 cal, 30 g fat, 113 mg chol, 566 mg sodium, 68 g carbo, 3 g fiber, 7 g pro.

Baked Apple Bowl Pies

Beneath a blanket of rich pastry lies a whole apple stuffed with caramel and hazelnuts. Skip the crimp and simply lay the pastry over the no-fuss whole apple, pinching slightly at the corners. Crunchy apples such as Granny Smiths, Braeburns and Jonathans are all delicious in this recipe.

PREP 45 minutes **BAKE** 30 minutes **STAND** 20 minutes

2 cups all-purpose flour
3 tablespoons sugar
½ teaspoon salt
¼ cup cold butter
¼ cup shortening
⅓ cup milk
1 egg, separated
2 tablespoons water
1 cup caramel ice cream topping
¼ cup chopped toasted hazelnuts*
½ teaspoon apple pie spice
8 small baking apples, cored and peeled
2 tablespoons butter, cut into 8 small pieces
1 lemon, cut in half
Ground cinnamon
Sage leaves (optional)

1. For pastry: In a large bowl, combine the flour, 3 tablespoons sugar and salt. Cut in ¼ cup butter and shortening until pieces are pea size. In a small bowl, combine milk, egg yolk and 1 tablespoon of the water. Add to flour mixture. Stir with a fork until combined. Gather mixture and knead gently until it forms a dough. Divide dough in half.

2. On a floured surface, roll each dough half into an 8x8-inch square, about ⅛ inch thick. Using a pizza cutter, cut each square into four 4-inch squares. Cover; set aside.

3. In a small bowl, combine ½ cup of the caramel topping, hazelnuts and apple pie spice. Place each apple in a 6-ounce ramekin. Fill each apple center with caramel mixture. Dot each with one piece of butter. Squeeze lemon halves over apples. Lay a pastry square over each apple, pinching corners with fingers. Arrange ramekins in a foil-lined 15x10x1-inch baking pan. In a small bowl, whisk together egg white and the remaining 1 tablespoon water. Brush over pastry.

4. Bake in a 350° about 30 minutes or until pastry is golden brown and apples are tender. Remove; let stand in pan on wire rack 20 minutes. Serve warm with remaining caramel sauce and a sprinkle of cinnamon. If you like, sprinkle with fresh sage leaves. **Makes 8 servings.**

Make-ahead directions: Cover apples with pastry squares, cover with plastic wrap and chill up to 24 hours. Cover and chill egg white. When ready to bake, prepare egg white mixture and proceed as directed.

*Tip: To toast hazelnuts, spread nuts in a single layer in a shallow baking pan. Bake in a 350° oven for 8 to 10 minutes or until lightly toasted, stirring once to toast evenly. Cool nuts slightly. Place the warm nuts on a clean kitchen towel; rub with the towel to remove the loose skins.

Per serving: 427 cal, 19 g fat, 47 mg chol, 292 mg sodium, 62 g carbo, 4 g fiber, 5 g pro.

Sharing is admirable, but when you serve these charming little desserts, no one has to! A cross between a pie and a dumpling, they're super simple to make.

Chocolate Pumpkin Cake

The whipped cream topping isn't as stable as buttercream frosting, so plan to assemble the cake just before serving.

PREP 1 hour **BAKE** 30 minutes **COOL** 2 hours **STAND** 2 hours, 5 minutes **CHILL** 1 hour

1 cup canned pumpkin
½ cup buttermilk
1½ cups all-purpose flour
⅔ cup unsweetened cocoa powder
2 teaspoons baking powder
1 teaspoon baking soda
½ teaspoon salt
¾ cup butter, softened
1 cup granulated sugar
1 cup packed brown sugar
1 tablespoon vanilla
4 eggs
¾ cup whipping cream
1 11.5-ounce package milk chocolate pieces
2 cups whipping cream
2 cups powdered sugar
2 teaspoons ground cinnamon
¼ teaspoon ground allspice
¾ cup canned pumpkin
4 drinking straws (optional)
  Chocolate curls or sprinkles

1. In a small bowl, combine 1 cup pumpkin and the buttermilk; set aside. In a medium bowl, whisk together flour, cocoa powder, baking powder, baking soda and salt; set aside.

2. In a large mixing bowl, beat butter, granulated sugar, brown sugar and vanilla on medium to high speed until light and fluffy. Add eggs, one at a time. Add flour mixture and pumpkin mixture alternately, beating on low speed to combine. Beat on medium to high speed for 20 seconds more. Spread batter into two greased and floured 8x8x2-inch square baking pans.

3. Bake in a 350° oven for 30 to 35 minutes or until a wooden toothpick inserted near centers comes out clean. Cool in pans on wire racks for 10 minutes. Remove cakes from pans; cool thoroughly on wire racks.

4. Meanwhile, prepare ganache. In a medium saucepan, bring ¾ cup cream just to boiling over medium-high heat. Remove from heat. Add chocolate pieces (do not stir). Let stand for 5 minutes. Stir until smooth. Let stand for 1 hour or until slightly thickened. Pour the ganache over the cool cake layers. (Place waxed paper under wire racks to catch drips.) Let stand for 1 to 2 hours, until ganache sets.

5. Meanwhile, prepare topping. In a chilled large mixing bowl, beat 2 cups cream, ½ cup powdered sugar, the cinnamon and allspice until soft peaks form. Fold in ¾ cup pumpkin and remaining powdered sugar. Beat on medium speed until stiff peaks form. Chill the topping for 1 hour.

6. To assemble, place one cake layer on a serving platter. If you like, insert four drinking straws to help support the top layer. Snip the straws with scissors about ¾ inch above the ganache. Spread about 2 cups topping over cake layer. Gently place second cake layer on top. Spoon remaining topping into a pastry bag fitted with a large open star tip. Pipe topping on cake in nine large swirls. Garnish with chocolate curls. Serve immediately; chill leftovers.
Makes 16 servings.

Per serving: 559 cal, 32 g fat, 133 mg chol, 350 mg sodium, 68 g carbo, 4 g fiber, 6 g pro.

Walnut Cake with Caramel Whipped Cream

PREP 25 minutes **BAKE** 35 minutes

    1 cup walnut halves or pieces
    ¾ cup unbleached all-purpose flour
    1 cup sugar
    1 medium orange
    ¼ teaspoon salt
    7 eggs, separated
    ½ teaspoon cream of tartar
      Caramel Whipped Cream (recipe follows)
      Simple Caramel Sauce (recipe, page 172)

1. In a food processor, combine walnuts and flour. Process until nuts are finely ground; set aside. Set aside 2 tablespoons of the sugar.

2. Finely zest and juice the orange. In a large bowl, combine the remaining sugar, 1 teaspoon of the orange zest, ⅓ cup of the orange juice, the salt and egg yolks. Beat with an electric mixer on high speed until very thick and pale, 3 to 5 minutes.

3. In another large clean, dry bowl and using clean, dry beaters, beat the egg whites and cream of tartar until soft peaks form (tips curl) when beaters are lifted. Gradually beat in the 2 tablespoons reserved sugar until egg whites are stiff (tips stand straight) but not dry.

4. Spoon about one-fourth of the beaten egg whites over yolk mixture. Add nut mixture. Fold together with a large rubber spatula. Add the remaining egg whites and fold to combine. Scrape batter into an ungreased 10-inch tube pan with removable bottom;

spread evenly in pan. Bake in a 325° oven for 35 to 40 minutes or until cake is golden brown, springy to the touch and a toothpick inserted near center comes out clean. Cool cake upside down in pan by inverting cake pan over a bottle with a long neck.

5. By the time the cake is cool, most will have pulled away from sides of pan; rap sides of pan sharply on counter to release any portion of cake that is still attached. Run a skewer or long thin spatula around tube to detach; lift to remove cake. Slide a thin spatula around bottom of cake to detach bottom.

6. Using a sharp serrated knife, cut cake into two layers. Fill layers with Caramel Whipped Cream. Serve with Simple Caramel Sauce. **Makes 12 servings.**

Per serving (with Caramel Whipped Cream and sauce): 541 cal, 31 g fat, 171 mg chol, 152 mg sodium, 62 g carbo, 2 g fiber, 9 g pro.

Caramel Whipped Cream

START TO FINISH 35 minutes

    ½ cup water
    1 cup sugar
    1⅓ cups coarsely chopped walnuts or pecans
    1 cup whipping cream

1. Line baking sheet with foil or parchment paper; set aside.

2. Place water in a 2-quart saucepan. Pour sugar in a thin stream in center of pan to form a low mound. Don't stir; use your fingers to pat sugar mound down until it

is entirely moistened. Any sugar touching edges of pan should be below the water line. Cook, covered, over medium heat for a few minutes, without stirring, until sugar is dissolved and syrup looks clear.

3. Uncover and continue to cook, without stirring, until syrup begins to color slightly. Swirl pan gently (rather than stirring) if syrup is coloring unevenly. Use a skewer to drop a bead of syrup on a plate from time to time. When a drop looks pale amber, add the nuts. Using a silicone spatula, gently turn nuts until they are completely coated with syrup.

4. Continue to cook, gently pushing nuts around if syrup is coloring unevenly, until a drop of syrup looks golden amber on the plate (about 30 minutes total). If syrup gets too dark, it will taste bitter. Immediately scrape mixture onto the lined baking sheet and spread it out as well as you can.

5. While still warm but cool enough to handle, break into pieces. Transfer to a resealable plastic bag. Keep airtight until needed so they will not become sticky.

6. When ready to use, break caramel into smaller pieces; chop to medium fine or pulse in food processor. In a large chilled bowl, beat cream with an electric mixer on medium speed until it holds soft peaks. Fold in chopped caramel. **Makes 12 servings (3 cups).**

Per serving: 110 cal, 8 g fat, 14 mg chol, 4 mg sodium, 10 g carbo, 0 g fiber, 1 g pro.

Simple Caramel Sauce

START TO FINISH 30 minutes

¾ cup whipping cream
2 tablespoons water
½ cup water
1 cup sugar
¼ teaspoon salt
1 teaspoon vanilla extract

1. In a small saucepan, heat cream and the 2 tablespoons water until steaming hot. Remove from heat; set aside.

2. Place the ½ cup water in a 2-quart saucepan; pour sugar and salt in a thin stream in center of pan to form a low mound. Don't stir; use your fingers to pat the sugar mound down until it is entirely moistened. Any sugar touching edges of pan should be below the water line. Cook, covered, over medium heat, without stirring, until sugar is dissolved and syrup looks clear.

3. Uncover and continue to cook, without stirring, until syrup begins to color slightly. Swirl pan gently (rather than stirring) if syrup is coloring unevenly. If syrup gets too dark, it will taste bitter. Use a skewer to drop a bead of syrup on a plate from time to time. When a drop of syrup looks amber, about 13 minutes, remove pan from heat. Holding pan away from you, gradually pour in the hot cream mixture. Stir over low heat to blend the caramel into the cream mixture. Simmer for 1 to 2 minutes.

4. Remove from heat; stir in vanilla. Let cool until slightly thickened (220° to 222°). Serve warm with Walnut Cake with Caramel Whipped Cream. Or store, tightly covered, in the refrigerator up to 1 week. **Makes 12 servings.**

Per serving: 71 cal, 3 g fat, 12 mg chol, 33 mg sodium, 10 g carbo, 0 g fiber, 0 g pro.

Cranberry Orange Upside-Down Spice Cake

PREP 20 minutes **BAKE** 35 minutes

1½ cups all-purpose flour
1 teaspoon baking powder
½ teaspoon ground ginger
½ teaspoon ground cinnamon
¼ teaspoon baking soda
¼ teaspoon salt
3 tablespoons butter
¾ cup packed brown sugar
1 11-ounce can mandarin orange sections, drained
1 cup fresh or frozen cranberries
2 eggs
¾ cup plain Greek yogurt or sour cream
¾ cup granulated sugar
6 tablespoons butter, melted
1 teaspoon vanilla

1. In a medium bowl, whisk together all-purpose flour, baking powder, ginger, cinnamon, baking soda and salt. Set aside. Place 3 tablespoons butter in a 10x2-inch cast-iron or other heavy ovengoing skillet. Place skillet in a 350° oven for 3 to 5 minutes to melt butter. Remove from oven and carefully tip skillet to coat the sides with butter. Leave oven on.

2. Sprinkle brown sugar evenly over the bottom of the skillet. Arrange orange sections, then cranberries, evenly over the brown sugar; set aside.

3. In a large bowl, whisk together eggs, yogurt, granulated sugar, melted butter and vanilla. Add flour mixture to egg mixture, one-third at a time, stirring just until combined after each addition. Spoon batter into skillet, spreading to cover fruit.

4. Bake in the 350° oven for 35 to 40 minutes or until a toothpick inserted into center of cake comes out clean. Let cake cool for 3 to 4 minutes. Loosen cake from pan; invert onto platter. Replace any fruit remaining in pan. Serve warm or at room temperature. **Makes 8 servings.**

Per serving: 408 cal, 15 g fat, 84 mg chol, 320 mg sodium, 63 g carbo, 2 g fiber, 6 g pro.

CRANBERRY
ORANGE UPSIDE-
DOWN SPICE CAKE

Caramel Pecan Skillet Brownie

PREP 25 minutes **BAKE** 35 minutes **COOL** 15 minutes

1 cup coarsely chopped pecans
¼ cup butter
½ cup packed brown sugar
½ cup whipping cream
1⅓ cups packed brown sugar
1 cup all-purpose flour
½ cup unsweetened cocoa powder
2 teaspoons instant coffee crystals
¾ teaspoon baking soda
½ teaspoon salt
4 eggs, lightly beaten
6 tablespoons butter, melted
¼ cup whipping cream
6 ounces dark chocolate, coarsely chopped
Coffee or vanilla ice cream (optional)

1. Heat a 10x2-inch cast-iron or other heavy oven-going skillet over medium-high heat. Add pecans; cook and stir for 2 to 3 minutes or until very lightly toasted. Add ¼ cup butter to skillet; stir to melt, then add ½ cup brown sugar. Cook and stir until mixture bubbles and sugar begins to melt. Remove from heat and carefully add ½ cup cream to skillet. Return to heat; cook and stir until combined and sugar is melted. Set aside.

2. In a medium bowl, combine 1⅓ cups brown sugar, the flour, cocoa powder, coffee crystals, baking soda and salt. Add eggs, 6 tablespoons melted butter and ¼ cup cream; stir until combined. Fold in chopped dark chocolate. Carefully spoon mixture over nut mixture in skillet.

3. Bake in a 325° oven for 35 minutes or until just set (place a shallow baking pan on the rack below to catch any drips). Remove from oven and cool slightly on a wire rack. If you like, serve warm with ice cream.
Makes 10 servings.

Per serving: 573 cal, 34 g fat, 130 mg chol, 361 mg sodium, 64 g carbo, 4 g fiber, 7 g pro.

Whether you're on two wheels or two legs, a fall afternoon with family is time well spent.

CORNMEAL PUMPKIN
CAKE WITH DRIED FRUIT
COMPOTE, PAGE 220

Winter

APPETIZERS, SNACKS & BEVERAGES

Candy Cane Popcorn Mix 208

Cranberry Margarita 180

Cucumber Bites with Herbed Cheese and Salmon Mousse 179

French Onion Sliders 185

Parmesan-Crusted Goat Cheese with Basil Oil 183

Sausage-and-Spinach-Stuffed Mushrooms 180

Sparkling Cranberry Brie Bites 179

Turkey Pesto Sliders 180

BREADS

Chocolate, Hazelnut and Maple Bacon Scones 208

Sweet Potato Biscuits 204

MAIN DISHES

Apple Harvest Chili 199

Bacon-Pear Macaroni and Cheese 199

Cider-Brined Turkey with Apples 195

Cinnamon-Spiced Beef Stroganoff 190

Grape-Stuffed Chicken with Lemon Orzo 196

Lemon-Rosemary Pork Loin with Cherry Sauce 192

Roasted Pork and Beet Salad 192

Sausage Polenta with Nestled Eggs 185

Spicy Beef, Bean and Vegetable Stew 189

SIDES

Braised Cabbage with Spicy Croutons 207

Broccoli-Cheese Soup 200

Calico Corn-Bread Dressing 207

Carrot-Ginger Soup 200

Cauliflower Gratin 203

Cranberry Chutney 204

Curried Cauliflower Soup 200

Lemony Green Beans 203

Maple-Butternut Puree 204

Pumpkin Parsnip Bisque with Hazelnut Toasts 200

SWEETS

Chocolate Cream Pie 215

Cornmeal Pumpkin Cake with Dried Fruit Compote 220

Decadent Chocolate-Peanut Butter Cheesecake 216

Eggnog Cheesecake Bars 230

Gingerbread Trifle 212

Gingered Fruitcake 223

Lemon-Vanilla Ornament Cookies 228

Nutella Cherry Hazelnut Fudge 230

Peppermint Sugar Cookies 227

Raspberry Truffles 230

Salty Caramel and Pecan Oatmeal Cookies 229

Spiced Chocolate-Pistachio Cookies 228

Toasted Fennel and Lemon Cake 224

Triple-Pear Pie with Walnut Crust 216

White Christmas Peppermint Layer Cake 219

SPARKLING
CRANBERRY
BRIE BITES

Sparkling Cranberry Brie Bites

Find easy-to-slice logs of Brie at large supermarkets.

PREP 45 minutes **STAND** 1 hour

24 round wheat crackers
3 ounces Brie cheese, thinly sliced
   Sugared Cranberries (recipe follows)

Place crackers on a serving platter. Top each cracker with a thin slice of Brie and garnish with three to four Sugared Cranberries. Serve immediately. **Makes 24 appetizers.**

Sugared Cranberries: Place a wire rack with small openings (so cranberries don't fall through) on a foil-lined baking sheet; set aside. In a small saucepan, combine ½ cup water and ½ cup sugar. Heat over medium-low heat, stirring occasionally, until the sugar is fully dissolved. Remove the pan from the heat and let cool slightly. Add 1 cup fresh cranberries to the saucepan and stir gently to coat. Using a slotted spoon or strainer, remove the cranberries from the sugar mixture and let drain. Place the cranberries on the rack. Let stand about 1 hour. Roll cranberries in additional sugar.

Per appetizer: 36 cal, 1 g fat, 4 mg chol, 46 mg sodium, 5 g carbo, 0 g fiber, 1 g pro.

Cucumber Bites with Herbed Cheese and Salmon Mousse

The recipe makes half the bites with pink salmon filling and half with white herbed cheese. If you like, streamline by choosing just one filling and doubling its ingredients.

START TO FINISH 30 minutes

8 ounces smoked salmon (lox-style)
1 8-ounce package cream cheese, softened
1 teaspoon dried dill weed
¼ teaspoon ground black pepper
1 clove garlic, finely minced
1 5.2-ounce package semisoft garlic and
   herb cheese (such as Boursin)
2 to 3 tablespoons whipping cream
2 medium cucumbers, peeled*

1. For Salmon Mousse: Combine salmon, cream cheese, dill, pepper and garlic in the bowl of a food processor. Cover and pulse until blended and smooth. Transfer mixture to a pastry bag fitted with a decorative tip; set aside.

2. For Herbed Cheese: Place semisoft cheese in a small bowl. Add 2 tablespoons heavy cream. Stir with a fork until lightened and smooth, adding additional cream if necessary to reach a piping consistency. Transfer mixture to a pastry bag fitted with a decorative tip; set aside.

3. Slice cucumber into ½-inch-thick slices. Scoop out most of the seeds from each slice, leaving a small portion to keep the filling from falling out. Arrange slices on a serving platter. Pipe a dollop of the salmon mousse or herbed cheese onto each cucumber slice. Can be chilled up to 6 hours before serving. **Makes 18 appetizers.**

*Tip: For a striped look, peel the length of the cucumber, leaving alternating peeled and unpeeled sections.

Per appetizer: 100 cal, 9 g fat, 27 mg chol, 344 mg sodium, 1 g carbo, 0 g fiber, 4 g pro.

When the holiday season arrives, it's nice to have a few recipes for quick-to-fix appetizers in your back pocket for last-minute entertaining.

Sausage-and-Spinach-Stuffed Mushrooms

This classic appetizer is always a hit at parties.

PREP 25 minutes **BAKE** 18 minutes

- 16 whole button mushrooms with 2-inch caps (about 12 ounces)
- 4 to 5 ounces bulk spicy Italian sausage (or one link, casing removed)
- 2 cloves garlic, minced
- ¼ teaspoon crushed red pepper (optional)
- 2 cups baby spinach leaves
- 1 egg
- 3 tablespoons panko bread crumbs
- ¼ teaspoon dried basil, crushed
- ⅛ teaspoon salt
  Dash ground black pepper
- 1 teaspoon olive oil

1. Clean mushroom caps with a damp paper towel. Remove the stems from caps. Coarsely chop stems and set aside.

2. Crumble sausage into a large skillet and cook over medium-high heat, stirring occasionally, until no longer pink. Stir in the chopped mushroom stems and continue to cook until they have released most of their juices, about 5 minutes. Stir in garlic and, if you like, crushed red pepper and cook just until fragrant, about 30 seconds more. Stir in spinach; cover and cook just until spinach is wilted, about 2 minutes. Transfer mixture to a food processor or blender. Cover and pulse to evenly chop mixture. Add the egg and pulse just until incorporated.

3. Fill each mushroom cap with about 1 tablespoon sausage mixture. Place filled caps on a foil-lined 15x10x1-inch baking pan. In a small bowl, stir together the panko, dried basil, salt and black pepper.

Add olive oil and toss to combine. Sprinkle some of the panko mixture over each stuffed mushroom. Bake in a 400° oven for 18 to 20 minutes or until topping is golden. **Makes 16 stuffed mushrooms.**

Per stuffed mushroom: 41 cal, 3 g fat, 17 mg chol, 83 mg sodium, 2 g carbo, 0 g fiber, 2 g pro.

Turkey Pesto Sliders

When you need a quick snack to serve drop-in guests, offer these little sandwiches that go together in 15 minutes or less.

PREP 15 minutes **BAKE** 8 minutes

- 6 slices turkey deli meat
- 6 slider buns, split horizontally
- 6 slices provolone cheese
- 3 tablespoons purchased basil pesto
- 3 tablespoons mayonnaise
- 1 tablespoon butter, melted

1. Lay a folded slice of turkey on the bottom half of each bun. Top each with a slice of provolone. (Tear turkey and cheese as necessary to fit.) In a small bowl, combine the pesto and mayonnaise. Spread a thin layer of pesto mixture on the insides of bun tops. Place on cheese.

2. Arrange sandwiches on a foil-lined baking sheet. Brush bun tops lightly with melted butter. Bake in a 400° oven for 8 to 10 minutes or until the cheese is melted and sandwiches are warmed through. **Makes 6 sliders.**

Per slider: 296 cal, 18 g fat, 48 mg chol, 613 mg sodium, 16 g carbo, 1 g fiber, 18 g pro.

Cranberry Margarita

The favorite cocktail of summer gets a winter twist—and a beautiful pink hue—from tart cranberry juice.

PREP 5 minutes **COOK** 10 minutes **CHILL** 30 minutes

- 1 cup cranberry juice
- ½ cup freshly squeezed lime juice
- ½ cup tequila
- ¼ cup triple sec (or other orange liqueur)
- 3 tablespoons Simple Syrup (recipe follows)
  Coarse sugar for rimming (optional)

Stir together cranberry and lime juices, tequila, triple sec and Simple Syrup. Serve over ice in glasses rimmed with coarse sugar, if you like. **Makes 3 servings.**

Simple Syrup: In a saucepan, combine equal parts granulated sugar and water. (A half cup of each makes enough syrup for about 15 margaritas.) Cook and stir over medium-high heat until sugar dissolves and mixture comes to a boil. Refrigerate until well chilled, about 30 minutes. Store in an airtight container in the refrigerator up to 2 months.

Per serving: 220 cal, 0 g fat, 0 mg chol, 13 mg sodium, 28 g carbo, 0 g fiber, 0 g pro.

Parmesan-Crusted Goat Cheese with Basil Oil

This recipe makes one small cheese ball, but easily doubles or triples to make multiple for a party.

START TO FINISH 25 minutes

½ ounce Parmesan cheese
¼ cup panko bread crumbs
Ground black pepper
¼ teaspoon coarse salt
1 clove garlic, minced
4 ounces semifirm plain goat cheese (chèvre)
¼ cup fresh basil leaves
1 clove garlic
¼ cup extra virgin olive oil
Fresh basil leaves (optional)
Baguette slices

1. Place the Parmesan in a small food processor. Pulse until finely ground. Add panko and pulse a few more times so the cheese and crumbs have an even, fine texture. Season to taste with pepper. Transfer to a shallow plate or bowl. Wipe out the bowl of the food processor.

2. Sprinkle the salt over the minced garlic in a small bowl and smash with a fork to form a paste. (Or sprinkle salt over minced garlic on cutting board and mash with the side of a chef's knife.) Crumble the goat cheese into the bowl with the garlic paste. Stir until smooth. Season to taste with salt and pepper. Form into a ball. Roll the ball in the Parmesan-panko mixture until well coated. Cover in plastic wrap and refrigerate until needed.

3. Meanwhile, bring a small saucepan of water to boiling. Add ¼ cup basil leaves and boil for 30 seconds. Drain and rinse immediately with cold water. Thoroughly blot the basil with a towel; place it in the food processor with one clove garlic. Pulse until finely minced. Scrape down sides of bowl. With food processor running, add oil through the feed tube in a steady stream. Continue processing until well blended. (The oil will take on a green hue.) Strain the oil mixture through a fine-mesh sieve onto a serving plate. Place cheese ball in the center. Garnish with additional fresh basil, if you like. Serve with baguette slices.
Makes 6 servings.

Per serving: 290 cal, 15 g fat, 17 mg chol, 624 mg sodium, 28 g carbo, 1 g fiber, 11 g pro.

Each December, the Victorian Sleighbell Parade and Old Christmas Weekend in Manistee, Michigan, sees the town of 6,220 swell to 10,000 revellers in search of food, shopping and fun.

FRENCH ONION
SLIDERS

French Onion Sliders

PREP 15 minutes COOK 24 minutes
BAKE 15 minutes

2 tablespoons unsalted butter
1 tablespoon olive oil
2 large yellow onions, halved and
    thinly sliced
¼ teaspoon kosher salt
⅛ teaspoon ground black pepper
    Pinch sugar
1½ teaspoons snipped fresh thyme leaves
    or ½ teaspoon dried thyme, crushed
¼ cup dry white wine or beef broth
24 baguette-style French bread slices,
    about ½ inch thick
1 to 2 cloves garlic, peeled and halved
6 ounces thinly sliced Gruyère cheese
2 tablespoons olive oil

1. Heat butter and 1 tablespoon oil in a large skillet over medium heat. When butter melts, add onions, salt, pepper and sugar to pan. Stir well, then reduce heat to medium-low. Cook, stirring occasionally, until onions are golden and caramelized, about 15 to 20 minutes. Stir in thyme; cook 1 minute more. Remove skillet from heat; add wine. Return skillet to stove; cook over medium-high heat, stirring frequently, until most of the liquid has evaporated. Remove from the heat; set aside.

2. Rub one side of each baguette slice with the cut side of a garlic clove. Layer 12 baguette slices with a bit of the sliced Gruyère, 2 to 3 teaspoons onion mixture and another slice or two of cheese. Place the remaining baguette slices on top. Lightly brush the tops with some of the remaining olive oil. Bake in a 400° oven for 15 minutes, flipping once and brushing with remaining olive oil halfway through baking. Serve warm. **Makes 12 sliders.**

Per slider: 178 cal, 10 g fat, 21 mg chol, 223 mg sodium, 15 g carbo, 1 g fiber, 7 g pro.

Sausage Polenta with Nestled Eggs

This Mexican-inspired breakfast casserole chills overnight and bakes in the morning, freeing you to relax with coffee and the paper.

PREP 35 minutes CHILL overnight BAKE 1 hour STAND 5 minutes

2½ cups vegetable broth
1¼ cups milk
1 cup quick-cooking polenta mix
1¼ cups shredded Mexican-style four-cheese
    blend (5 ounces)
1 4-ounce can diced green chiles, undrained
8 ounces bulk pork sausage
2 cups sliced fresh mushrooms
1 cup finely chopped onion
    Nonstick cooking spray
8 eggs
    Ground black pepper (optional)
    Snipped fresh cilantro (optional)
    Bottled hot pepper sauce (optional)

1. In a large saucepan, bring broth to boiling. Meanwhile, in a small bowl, stir together milk and polenta. Add polenta mixture in a slow, steady stream to broth, stirring constantly; reduce heat. Cook and stir until bubbly; cook and stir for 3 to 5 minutes more, until polenta thickens. Stir in cheese and chiles; set aside.

2. In a very large skillet, cook sausage, mushrooms and onion over medium-high heat until meat is browned and onion is tender. Drain and discard liquid. Stir in polenta mixture.

3. Spread polenta-meat mixture in a greased 3-quart oval or rectangular baking dish. Cover with greased or nonstick foil; chill overnight.

4. While oven preheats to 375°, use the bottom of a ⅓-cup measuring cup coated with cooking spray to make eight indentations in the polenta-meat mixture. Bake, covered, for 35 minutes. Reduce oven temperature to 325°. Remove dish from oven; remove foil. Break one egg into a small, shallow bowl. Slide egg into an indentation. Repeat with remaining eggs. Return to oven.

5. Bake, uncovered, in the 325° oven for 25 minutes or until the eggs are almost set. Let stand on wire rack 5 to 10 minutes (eggs will continue to cook). If you like, sprinkle with black pepper and cilantro and serve with hot pepper sauce. **Makes 8 servings.**

Per serving: 392 cal, 19 g fat, 225 mg chol, 686 mg sodium, 34 g carbo, 4 g fiber, 20 g pro.

For 25 years, the turn-of-the-20th-century buildings of downtown Manistee, Michigan, have stood witness to the arrival of the town's towering Christmas tree, the centerpiece of its Victorian Sleighbell Parade and Old Christmas Weekend.

Spicy Beef, Bean and Vegetable Stew

Affordable beef chuck roast, apple, parsnip and sweet potato slow-simmer in broth flavored with dark beer, herbs and spices. Warm corn bread muffins and cold winter night optional.

PREP 20 minutes **COOK** 1 hour 40 minutes

1 pound boneless beef chuck pot roast
2 tablespoons olive oil or vegetable oil
1 cup coarsely chopped onion (1 large)
3 cloves garlic, minced
2 14.5-ounce cans reduced-sodium beef broth
1 12-ounce bottle dark beer (such as stout, porter or lager) or 1½ cups reduced-sodium beef broth
2 to 3 teaspoons bottled hot pepper sauce
1½ teaspoons dried oregano, crushed
½ teaspoon ground allspice
1 teaspoon sea or kosher salt
2 bay leaves
1 large sweet potato, peeled and cut into 1-inch pieces (about 1½ cups)
2 medium parsnips, peeled, halved lengthwise and cut into 1-inch pieces (about 1¼ cups)
2 medium carrots, halved lengthwise and cut into 1-inch pieces (about 1 cup)
1 cup coarsely chopped, peeled firm, tart apple (1 large)
1 15.5-ounce can butter beans, rinsed and drained
1 4-ounce can diced green chiles, undrained
Corn bread muffins (optional)

1. Trim fat from meat; cut into 1-inch pieces. Pat meat dry with paper towels. In a 5- to 6-quart Dutch oven, cook half the meat in 1 tablespoon of the hot oil over medium heat, turning to brown evenly. Using a slotted spoon, remove meat from pan. Add remaining oil and meat, chopped onion and garlic to pan. Cook until meat is browned and onion is tender. Drain fat. Return all meat to pan.

2. Add beef broth, beer, hot pepper sauce, oregano, allspice, salt and bay leaves. Bring to boiling; reduce heat. Simmer, covered, for 60 to 75 minutes or until meat is nearly tender.

3. Stir in sweet potato, parsnips, carrots, apple, beans and green chiles. Return to boiling; reduce heat. Simmer, covered, about 30 minutes more or until meat and vegetables are tender. Discard bay leaves. If you like, serve stew with corn bread muffins. **Makes 6 to 8 servings.**

Per serving: 312 cal, 8 g fat, 49 mg chol, 896 mg sodium, 36 g carbo, 7 g fiber, 24 g pro.

Visitors to Crystal Mountain Resort and Spa in Thompsonville, Michigan, can ski, get pampered, enjoy fine dining—or simply soak in the serenity.

Cinnamon-Spiced Beef Stroganoff

A touch of cinnamon infuses this classic dish with its sweet, warm flavor. If you like your food zippy, use the larger amount of cayenne pepper.

PREP 25 minutes **COOK** 20 minutes

1 pound boneless beef sirloin steak
¾ teaspoon salt
¾ teaspoon ground cinnamon
¼ teaspoon ground coriander
⅛ to ¼ teaspoon cayenne pepper
   Dash ground cloves
3 tablespoons butter
1 tablespoon all-purpose flour
1 cup reduced-sodium beef broth
¼ cup sour cream
1 teaspoon Dijon-style mustard
¼ teaspoon freshly ground black pepper
2 tablespoons olive oil
½ cup finely chopped shallots or finely
   chopped white onion
1 clove garlic, minced
4 cups sliced mushrooms (9 ounces)
   Cooked and buttered wide egg noodles

1. If you like, partially freeze beef for easier slicing. Trim fat from the meat and thinly slice across the grain into bite-size strips. Pat dry with paper towels; transfer meat to a bowl. Add ½ teaspoon of the salt, the cinnamon, coriander, cayenne pepper and cloves. Toss to coat evenly; set aside.

2. In a small saucepan, melt 1 tablespoon of the butter. Stir in flour until smooth. Cook over medium heat, stirring constantly, about 2 minutes, until light brown. Whisking constantly, add broth. Bring to boiling; reduce heat. Simmer, uncovered, for 3 minutes, whisking occasionally. Reduce heat to low; stir in sour cream, mustard, the remaining ¼ teaspoon salt and the ¼ teaspoon black pepper (do not boil). Cover and set aside.

3. In a heavy very large skillet, heat 1 tablespoon of the oil and 1 tablespoon of the remaining butter over medium-high heat. Cook meat, half at a time, in the oil mixture for 1 to 2 minutes or until meat browns on all sides but is still pink inside. Using a slotted spoon, remove meat from skillet to a medium bowl. Set aside.

4. Add the remaining 1 tablespoon of oil and 1 tablespoon of butter to the skillet; heat until hot but not smoking. Add shallots and garlic. Cook and stir for 3 minutes. Add mushrooms. Cook, stirring occasionally, for 8 to 10 minutes until liquid evaporates, mushrooms are browned, and shallots are soft and golden. Return meat and juices to skillet; stir to heat through. Pour sauce over meat mixture. Serve over noodles. **Makes 6 servings.**

Per serving: 356 cal, 18 g fat, 98 mg chol, 490 mg sodium, 20 g carbo, 2 g fiber, 29 g pro.

Roasted Pork and Beet Salad

PREP 20 minutes **COOK** 5 minutes **ROAST** 20 minutes **STAND** 3 minutes

    3 medium beets, trimmed, peeled and
        cut into 1-inch-thick wedges (about
        12 ounces)
  ⅜ teaspoon salt
  ¼ teaspoon ground black pepper
  ¼ teaspoon ground allspice
    1 12- to 16-ounce pork tenderloin,
        trimmed of fat
    2 teaspoons walnut oil or olive oil
    6 cups packaged fresh baby spinach
    2 medium apples, cored and chopped
    2 small shallots, thinly sliced
  ¼ cup chopped walnuts, toasted
        Orange Dressing (recipe follows)

1. In a medium saucepan, cook beets in a small amount of boiling water for 5 minutes; drain.

2. Meanwhile, rub ¼ teaspoon salt, the pepper and allspice evenly over pork. Place pork on one half of a foil-lined shallow roasting pan. Add beets to other half. Drizzle beets with oil and sprinkle with remaining ⅛ teaspoon salt. Toss beets to coat; spread evenly.

3. Roast, uncovered, in a 425° oven for 20 to 25 minutes or until an instant-read thermometer inserted in center of pork registers 145° and beets are tender. Cover pork with foil; let rest for 3 minutes. (While pork and beets roast, prepare Orange Dressing.)

4. To serve, thinly slice pork. Divide spinach among four plates. Top with pork, beets, apples, shallots and walnuts. Drizzle with Orange Dressing. **Makes 4 servings.**

Orange Dressing: In a screw-top jar, combine 2 teaspoons orange zest, ⅓ cup orange juice, ¼ cup walnut or olive oil, 2 tablespoons snipped fresh chives or finely chopped shallot, 1 tablespoon honey, 2 teaspoons horseradish mustard and ⅛ teaspoon salt. Cover the jar; shake well.

Per serving: 403 cal, 23 g fat, 52 mg chol, 458 mg sodium, 31 g carbo, 7 g fiber, 22 g pro.

Lemon-Rosemary Pork Loin with Cherry Sauce

PREP 30 minutes **ROAST** 45 minutes
STAND 10 minutes

    4 cloves garlic, minced
    1 teaspoon lemon zest
    1 tablespoon lemon juice
    1 tablespoon olive oil
    1 tablespoon Dijon-style coarse-
        ground mustard
    1 tablespoon snipped fresh rosemary
  ½ teaspoon salt
  ⅛ teaspoon ground black pepper
    1 pound boneless pork top loin roast
        (single loin)
  ½ cup cranberry, cherry or apple juice
  ¼ cup red currant jelly
    2 teaspoons cornstarch
    1 teaspoon Dijon-style coarse-
        ground mustard
    1 cup fresh sweet cherries, halved and
        pitted, or 1 cup frozen unsweetened
        pitted dark sweet cherries, thawed

1. In a small bowl, combine garlic, lemon zest, lemon juice, olive oil, 1 tablespoon mustard, the rosemary, salt and pepper. Spread mixture over pork and place on a rack in a shallow roasting pan.

2. Roast, uncovered, in a 375° oven 45 to 55 minutes or until instant-read thermometer inserted in roast registers 145°. Transfer to a platter. Cover with foil. Let stand 10 minutes before carving.

3. Meanwhile, in a small saucepan, stir the cranberry juice, jelly, cornstarch and 1 teaspoon mustard over medium heat until thickened and bubbly. Cook and stir for 1 minute more, whisking constantly. Reduce heat to low. Add the cherries; stir until mixture is heated through. Serve with sliced pork roast. **Makes 4 servings.**

Per serving: 335 cal, 12 g fat, 80 mg chol, 464 mg sodium, 28 g carbo, 1 g fiber, 27 g pro.

LEMON-ROSEMARY
PORK LOIN WITH
CHERRY SAUCE

Cider-Brined Turkey with Apples

Brining the turkey—soaking it for at least 8 hours in a solution of water, salt, brown sugar, onions, garlic, ginger, peppercorns and citrus peel—infuses it with flavor and keeps it especially juicy after roasting.

PREP 30 minutes **BRINE** 8 hours **ROAST** 2 hours 45 minutes

½ gallon apple cider
3 quarts water
1 cup kosher salt
¾ cup packed brown sugar
2 medium onions, sliced ¼ inch thick
8 cloves garlic, crushed
8 ¼-inch-thick slices fresh ginger
2 tablespoons black peppercorns
1 orange
12 cups ice cubes
1 10- to 12-pound turkey
2 medium onions, sliced ¼ inch thick
8 sprigs fresh thyme
1 cup chicken broth
½ cup apple cider
⅓ cup Calvados (apple brandy) or apple cider
2 tablespoons cider vinegar
2 tablespoons butter
2 tablespoons snipped fresh sage
8 small cooking apples, cored, top thirds of apples peeled (2 pounds)
  Chicken broth
¼ cup all-purpose flour
  Fresh sage (optional)

1. For brine: In a 10-quart stockpot, combine ½ gallon cider, the water, salt, brown sugar, two onions, garlic, ginger and peppercorns. Using a peeler, remove wide strips of peel from orange and add to pot. Reserve the orange. Bring mixture to a simmer over medium-high heat, stirring occasionally. Remove from heat. Add ice.

2. Remove neck, gizzards and liver from turkey body cavity; discard or reserve for another use. Rinse cavity. Add turkey to brine. Place a pie plate on turkey to keep it submerged. Cover and refrigerate for 8 to 12 hours.

3. Remove turkey from brine; discard brine. Drain turkey and pat dry. Cut reserved orange into wedges and place in cavity. Tuck neck skin under back. Tuck drumsticks under band of skin at tail or provided wire or nylon clamp. Or tie drumsticks together with kitchen string. Twist wings under back.

4. Arrange the other two sliced onions and thyme in a large roasting pan. Place turkey, breast side up, on a rack in the pan. Add 1 cup chicken broth to pan.

5. Roast turkey in a 325° oven, uncovered, for 2¾ to 3 hours or until 175° when tested with an instant-read thermometer in the center of inside thigh muscles. If necessary to prevent overbrowning, tent turkey with foil the last 1 hour of roasting.

6. Meanwhile, combine ½ cup cider, the Calvados, vinegar, butter and 2 tablespoons sage in a small saucepan. Warm over low heat until butter melts; keep warm. After the turkey has roasted 1½ hours, begin brushing it occasionally with the butter mixture.

7. After the turkey has been roasting 2 hours, add apples to pan, bottoms down. Roast for 45 to 60 minutes or until apples are just tender. Spoon butter mixture over apples and turkey two or three more times or until mixture is all used. Continue basting apples and turkey with pan juices. If apples are done before turkey, transfer to serving dish and tent with foil.

8. Transfer turkey to platter and tent loosely with foil. While turkey rests, pour drippings into a heatproof 4-cup glass measure, leaving onions and other solids in pan. Skim fat from drippings. Return 4 tablespoons of fat to pan and discard remaining. If needed, add additional chicken broth to equal 3 cups drippings.

9. Place roasting pan over two burners set at medium-high heat. Add flour; cook and stir for 2 minutes. Add the 3 cups drippings to pan. Cook and stir with a whisk until mixture comes to a boil. Cook and stir for 2 to 3 minutes or until desired thickness. Strain into a serving bowl.

10. Arrange apples around turkey and serve with gravy. If you like, garnish with fresh sage. **Makes 12 servings.**

Per serving: 522 cal, 18 g fat, 255 mg chol, 768 mg sodium, 16 g carbo, 2 g fiber, 69 g pro.

Grape-Stuffed Chicken with Lemon Orzo

Fruit-and-nut stuffing transforms everyday chicken breasts into a company-ready feast. Bonus: It's deceptively simple; you'll have dinner on the table in an hour.

PREP 25 minutes **COOK** 9 minutes **BAKE** 15 minutes

4 skinless, boneless chicken breast halves (6 to 7 ounces each)
½ cup freshly grated Parmesan cheese
½ cup purple and/or red seedless grapes, quartered
¼ cup finely chopped toasted pecans
2 tablespoons butter, softened
2 tablespoons thinly sliced green onion (1)
½ teaspoon dried rosemary, crushed
¼ teaspoon ground cardamom
¼ teaspoon lemon-pepper seasoning
Sea or kosher salt
Freshly ground black pepper
2 tablespoons olive oil
1 cup dried orzo
1 teaspoon lemon zest
1 tablespoon lemon juice
¼ cup snipped Italian (flat-leaf) parsley
Lemon wedges (optional)

1. Using a sharp knife, cut a pocket in each chicken breast by cutting horizontally through the thickest portion to, but not through, the opposite side.

2. In a small bowl, combine ¼ cup of the cheese, the grapes, pecans, butter, green onion, rosemary, cardamom and lemon-pepper. Spoon filling into each pocket. Secure with two or three toothpicks through the open edges of the chicken to keep the filling from falling out. Sprinkle stuffed chicken breasts on both sides with salt and black pepper.

3. In a large cast-iron skillet or an oven-going skillet, heat 1 tablespoon of the oil over medium-high heat. Add stuffed chicken and cook for 4 to 5 minutes or until the bottoms are golden. Turn and cook for 5 minutes more.

4. Bake, uncovered, in a 350° oven for 15 to 18 minutes or until chicken is done (170°). Remove the toothpicks before serving.

5. Meanwhile, prepare orzo. Cook orzo according to package directions; drain. Return orzo to hot pan; toss with the remaining 1 tablespoon oil, the remaining ¼ cup cheese, the lemon zest, lemon juice and parsley. Serve hot with chicken; if you like, slice chicken breast before serving to reveal stuffing. Spoon pan juices over chicken and, if you like, garnish with lemon wedges. **Makes 4 servings.**

Per serving: 500 cal, 24 g fat, 95 mg chol, 430 mg sodium, 37 g carbo, 3 g fiber, 34 g pro.

A couple keeps the cold at bay at one of the outdoor fire pits at Crystal Mountain Resort and Spa in Thompsonville, Michigan.

BACON-PEAR MACARONI
AND CHEESE

Bacon-Pear Macaroni and Cheese

PREP 40 minutes **BAKE** 30 minutes **STAND** 10 minutes

8 ounces dried elbow macaroni or other short tubular pasta (about 2 cups)
6 slices bacon
½ cup chopped onion (1 medium)
2 cloves garlic, minced
2 tablespoons all-purpose flour
1 teaspoon dry mustard
½ teaspoon freshly ground black pepper
2½ cups whole milk
6 ounces smoked Gouda cheese, rind removed and shredded
1 8-ounce package cream cheese, cubed and softened
2 tablespoons snipped fresh oregano or 1 teaspoon dried oregano, crushed
2 tablespoons butter or margarine
2 tablespoons packed brown sugar
2 red and/or green pears, thinly sliced
2 tablespoons finely shredded Parmesan cheese

1. Cook pasta according to package directions; drain. Return pasta to hot pan; cover to keep warm. Set aside.

2. Meanwhile, in a large skillet, cook bacon over medium heat until crisp, turning once. Reserving 3 tablespoons drippings in skillet, drain bacon on paper towels. Crumble bacon and set aside.

3. Cook onion and garlic in drippings over medium heat for 30 seconds. Stir in flour, dry mustard and pepper. Add milk. Stir until thickened and bubbly; reduce heat. Add smoked Gouda and cream cheese; cook and stir until almost melted.

4. Pour cheese sauce over the pasta; stir in oregano and all but 2 tablespoons of the bacon. Transfer mixture to a 2-quart rectangular baking dish; cover with foil. Bake in a 350° oven for 25 minutes.

5. Meanwhile, melt butter in a clean large skillet. Stir in brown sugar; add pears. Cook, turning occasionally, until pears are tender, about 6 to 8 minutes. Remove from heat. Remove macaroni and cheese from oven. Remove foil from baking dish; stir about half of the sliced cooked pears into the pasta. Arrange the remaining pear slices over the pasta; sprinkle with Parmesan and reserved bacon. Bake 5 minutes more or until Parmesan has softened. Let stand 10 minutes before serving. **Makes 6 servings.**

Per serving: 586 cal, 33 g fat, 104 mg chol, 649 mg sodium, 52 g carbo, 3 g fiber, 22 g pro.

Apple Harvest Chili

START TO FINISH 45 minutes

1 16-ounce jar thick and chunky salsa
1 15- to 16-ounce can yellow hominy, rinsed and drained
1 15- to 16-ounce can black beans, rinsed and drained
1 14.5-ounce can reduced-sodium chicken broth
1 Granny Smith apple, chopped
⅔ cup dried cranberries, golden raisins or snipped dried apricots
1 tablespoon unsweetened cocoa powder
2 to 3 teaspoons chili powder
Several dashes chipotle-flavor bottled hot pepper sauce
⅔ cup coarsely chopped cashews
Garnish: Finely slivered or chopped Granny Smith apple and/or lime wedges (optional)

1. In a 4- or 5-quart Dutch oven, combine all ingredients except cashews and garnishes. Bring to boiling; reduce heat. Simmer, covered, for 20 minutes.

2. Just before serving, stir in cashews. If you like, garnish bowls with slivered apple or a lime wedge. **Makes 4 to 5 servings.**

Per serving: 395 cal, 13 g fat, 0 mg chol, 1,485 mg sodium, 67 g carbo, 13 g fiber, 13 g pro.

Curried Cauliflower Soup

Simmering for hours is so Sunday afternoon. On weeknights, whip up this light, budget-friendly soup.

START TO FINISH 25 minutes

2 tablespoons chopped celery
2 tablespoons chopped onion
2 tablespoons butter or margarine
4 teaspoons all-purpose flour
1 teaspoon curry powder
½ teaspoon instant chicken bouillon
    granules
    Pinch salt
    Pinch ground black pepper
2 cups milk
    Dash Worcestershire sauce
1 cup cooked cauliflower, chopped

1. In a heavy medium saucepan, cook celery and onion in butter until tender. Stir in flour, curry powder, bouillon granules, salt and pepper until blended. Add milk and Worcestershire sauce. Cook and stir until thickened and bubbly, then cook and stir for 1 minute more.

2. Cool slightly; add vegetables and blend with an immersion blender. (Or transfer vegetables and milk mixture to a blender; blend until smooth.) Return soup to saucepan; heat through. **Makes 2 servings.**

Per serving: 247 cal, 16 g fat, 18 mg chol, 618 mg sodium, 17 g carbo, 0 g fiber, 9 g pro.

Carrot-Ginger Soup: Prepare as directed, except substitute chopped cooked carrots for the cauliflower and omit curry powder. Add a pinch of ground ginger or ground nutmeg before blending. If you like, top with chopped peanuts.

Broccoli-Cheese Soup: Prepare as directed, except substitute broccoli for cauliflower and omit curry powder. Add 2 tablespoons grated cheddar cheese and a pinch of garlic salt before blending.

Pumpkin Parsnip Bisque with Hazelnut Toasts

Puree wintry veggies like potato, leek and parsnip into a velvety soup. Don't skip the crisp, buttery dippers.

PREP 45 minutes **COOK** 20 minutes **COOL** 5 minutes **BAKE** 3 minutes

1 tablespoon butter
2 medium leeks, halved lengthwise, rinsed
    and sliced crosswise (white and light
    green parts only) (⅔ cup)
1 stalk celery, chopped
½ teaspoon salt
⅛ teaspoon crushed red pepper
4 medium parsnips, peeled and cut into
    1-inch pieces (3 cups)
1 large russet potato, peeled and cut into
    2-inch chunks
4½ cups chicken stock or broth
1 15-ounce can pumpkin
¼ teaspoon ground allspice
⅓ cup sour cream
1 tablespoon lemon juice
    Hazelnut Toasts (recipe follows)

1. In a large saucepan, heat 1 tablespoon butter over medium-high heat until bubbling. Add leeks, celery, salt and crushed red pepper; cook and stir for 4 minutes, until vegetables start to soften.

2. Add parsnips, potato and chicken stock. Bring to boiling; reduce heat. Cover and cook for 20 to 30 minutes or until very tender, stirring occasionally. Stir in pumpkin and allspice. Remove soup from heat and let cool for 5 to 10 minutes.

3. Place soup, in batches if necessary, in a blender or food processor. Puree until smooth; return to saucepan. Add additional chicken stock to reach desired consistency. Stir sour cream and lemon juice into soup and heat through. Serve with Hazelnut Toasts. **Makes 8 servings.**

Make-ahead directions: Prepare soup as directed, except do not add sour cream or lemon juice. Soup can be refrigerated up to 3 days or frozen up to 1 month. Defrost and heat over medium-low heat before continuing with Step 3. Serve as directed.

Hazelnut Toasts: Stir ¼ cup toasted (see tip, page 167) and finely chopped hazelnuts into 3 tablespoons softened butter. Spread mixture over 16 toasted slices of baguette-style French bread. (At this point, toasts can stand at room temperature up to 2 hours before baking.) When ready to serve, bake toasts in a 300° oven for 3 to 5 minutes or until warm and butter is melted.

Per serving: 208 cal, 10 g fat, 19 mg chol, 562 mg sodium, 26 g carbo, 5 g fiber, 4 g pro.

PUMPKIN PARSNIP BISQUE
WITH HAZELNUT TOASTS

CAULIFLOWER GRATIN

Cauliflower Gratin

PREP 25 minutes **BAKE** 15 minutes

　1 cup panko bread crumbs
　3 ounces white cheddar cheese, finely
　　　shredded (¾ cup)
　2 tablespoons snipped fresh parsley
　2 teaspoons snipped fresh thyme
1½ teaspoons orange zest
　1 large head cauliflower, cut into small
　　　florets (about 6 cups)
　2 tablespoons olive oil
　2 tablespoons Dijon-style mustard
　¼ to ½ teaspoon salt
　2 tablespoons butter, melted
　¼ cup chopped roasted almonds

1. In a small bowl, combine panko, cheese, parsley, thyme and orange zest; set aside.

2. In a 4-quart pot, cook cauliflower in lightly salted boiling water for 4 minutes or until tender but still firm. Drain well.

3. In a large bowl, combine olive oil, mustard and salt. Add cauliflower and stir gently to coat. Transfer to a 1½- to 2-quart au gratin or rectangular baking dish.* Sprinkle with panko mixture. Drizzle with melted butter.

4. Bake on top rack of a 425° oven for 15 minutes or until heated through and lightly browned. Top with almonds. **Makes 6 servings.**

***Make-ahead directions:** At this point, the cauliflower and panko mixtures can be covered and refrigerated for up to 1 day. Remove from refrigerator 45 minutes before baking and continue with Step 3.

Per serving: 326 cal, 16 g fat, 25 mg chol, 370 mg sodium, 40 g carbo, 3 g fiber, 7 g pro.

Lemony Green Beans

PREP 25 minutes **COOK** 10 minutes

　2 pounds fresh green beans, trimmed
　3 tablespoons olive oil
　3 medium shallots, thinly sliced
　4 cloves garlic, thinly sliced
　½ teaspoon salt
　¼ teaspoon cracked black pepper
　2 teaspoons lemon zest (set aside)
　3 tablespoons fresh lemon juice

1. In a large heavy pot, cook beans in boiling lightly salted water for 4 minutes, until just crisp-tender. Drain; submerge in a bowl of ice water. Drain well.*

2. In the same pot, heat oil for 1 minute over medium-high heat. Add shallots, garlic, salt and pepper. Cook and stir for 2 minutes or until just softened. Add green beans and cook and stir for 4 minutes or until heated through. Add lemon juice; cook and stir until well coated. Transfer to a serving dish. Sprinkle with lemon zest. **Makes 6 servings.**

***Make-ahead directions:** At this point, the beans can be chilled, covered, for up to 1 day. Remove from refrigerator 45 minutes before serving. Continue with Step 2.

Per cup: 113 cal, 7 g fat, 0 mg chol, 203 mg sodium, 12 g carbo, 4 g fiber, 3 g pro.

Stained-glass windows brighten the facade of the 1891 Guardian Angels Church in historic Manistee, Michigan.

Maple-Butternut Puree

PREP 25 minutes **BAKE** 40 minutes

 2 tablespoons olive oil
 1 large butternut squash (2½ to 3 pounds)
 3 tablespoons butter, softened
 3 tablespoons maple syrup
 1½ teaspoons fresh thyme leaves
 ½ teaspoon salt
 ¼ teaspoon freshly grated nutmeg
 ¼ cup pepitas (pumpkin seeds), toasted
   Maple syrup (optional)

1. Brush a 15x10x1-inch baking sheet with the olive oil. Cut butternut squash in half lengthwise and remove seeds. Place squash, cut sides down, in pan. Bake, uncovered, in a 375° oven about 40 minutes or until very tender when pierced with a sharp knife. Remove from oven.

2. Meanwhile, in a large bowl, combine butter, 3 tablespoons syrup, thyme, salt and nutmeg. When squash is cool enough to handle, use a spoon to scrape flesh from skin into bowl with butter mixture.

3. In batches, puree mixture in a food processor or blender until smooth.*

4. Transfer to a serving dish and top with pepitas. Drizzle with a little additional maple syrup, if you like. **Makes 6 servings.**

*Make-ahead directions: The puree can be kept warm in a heavy covered saucepan over low heat, stirring occasionally, or refrigerated, covered, for up to 1 day and reheated over medium-low heat in a covered heavy saucepan. Stir occasionally.

Per cup: 243 cal, 15 g fat, 15 mg chol, 276 mg sodium, 27 g carbo, 4 g fiber, 4 g pro.

Cranberry Chutney

PREP 20 minutes **COOK** 10 minutes

 1 navel orange
 ¾ cup packed brown sugar
 ¼ cup cider vinegar
 ¼ cup water
 ⅓ cup finely chopped red onion
 4 ¼-inch-thick slices fresh ginger
 1 teaspoon mustard seeds
 ¼ teaspoon salt
 ⅛ teaspoon crushed red pepper
 1 12-ounce package cranberries, rinsed
 1 Granny Smith apple, peeled and chopped

1. Zest orange (should have 1 tablespoon); set aside. Cut ¼ inch off the top and bottom of the orange. With a sharp knife, remove skin and white membrane from orange. Working over a medium saucepan (to catch juice), separate and remove orange segments. Cut segments into small pieces and set aside. Squeeze remaining membrane over pan to extract any remaining juice.

2. Add brown sugar, vinegar, water, onion, ginger, mustard seeds, salt and crushed red pepper to saucepan. Bring to boiling over medium-high heat. Add cranberries and orange zest. Return to boiling; reduce heat. Cook, uncovered, for 7 minutes, stirring occasionally. Add apple. Cook about 3 minutes more or until apple is just tender.

3. Remove from heat, remove and discard ginger and stir in orange segments. Serve warm or refrigerate, covered, for up to 2 days. Bring to room temperature before serving. **Makes 6 servings (3 cups).**

Per serving: 163 cal, 0 g fat, 0 g chol, 107 mg sodium, 41 g carbo, 4 g fiber, 1 g pro.

Sweet Potato Biscuits

PREP 20 minutes **BAKE** 15 minutes

 2½ cups all-purpose flour
 2 tablespoons packed brown sugar
 1 tablespoon baking powder
 1 teaspoon salt
 ¼ teaspoon freshly grated nutmeg
 6 tablespoons cold butter, cut up
 1 cup mashed cooked sweet potato
 ¾ cup buttermilk
 1 teaspoon orange zest
 2 tablespoons butter, melted
 ½ teaspoon smoked paprika

1. In a large bowl, combine flour, brown sugar, baking powder, salt and nutmeg. Using a pastry blender, cut butter into flour until mixture resembles coarse crumbs. In a medium bowl, combine sweet potato, buttermilk and orange zest.*

2. Make a well in the center of the dry ingredients. Add liquid mixture. Using a fork, stir until mixture is moistened.

3. Knead dough in bowl about five times or until dough holds together. Transfer dough to a baking sheet lined with parchment paper. Roll or pat dough into an 8x8-inch square about ¾ inch thick. Using a sharp large knife, cut into 16 squares. Separate squares so they are about 1 inch apart.

4. In a small bowl, combine melted butter and paprika. Brush mixture over biscuits. Bake in a 425° oven for 15 minutes or until golden and edges appear dry. Remove from baking sheet. Serve warm. **Makes 16 biscuits.**

*Make-ahead directions: At this point, you can cover both bowls and refrigerate up to 8 hours before continuing with Step 2.

Per biscuit: 150 cal, 6 g fat, 16 mg chol, 306 mg sodium, 21 g carbo, 1 g fiber, 3 g pro.

CALICO CORN
BREAD DRESSING

Calico Corn-Bread Dressing

PREP 1 hour **BAKE** 32 minutes

12 ounces shiitake mushrooms
2¼ cups chicken broth
8 sprigs fresh thyme
1 sprig fresh sage
¼ teaspoon cracked black pepper
½ cup coarsely chopped onion (1 medium)
1 cup chopped carrot (2 medium)
1 cup thinly sliced celery (1 cup)
3 tablespoons olive oil
½ teaspoon salt
Corn Bread, coarsely crumbled (recipe follows)*
⅓ cup dried apricots, cut into strips
3 tablespoons snipped fresh Italian (flat-leaf) parsley
1 tablespoon snipped fresh sage

1. Remove stems from mushrooms. Put stems in a small saucepan with chicken broth, thyme, sage sprig and pepper. Bring to a simmer over medium-low heat.

2. Meanwhile, slice mushroom tops ¼ inch thick. Place mushroom tops, onion, carrot and celery in a 3-quart rectangular baking dish. Drizzle vegetables with oil and sprinkle with salt; stir to coat. Roast, uncovered, in a 425° oven for 15 to 18 minutes or until just tender and beginning to brown, stirring once.

3. Remove baking dish from oven; add crumbled Corn Bread, apricots, parsley and snipped sage. Stir until combined. Using a slotted spoon, remove mushroom stems, thyme stems and sage sprig from broth and drizzle over corn bread mixture.**

4. Bake, uncovered, in a 425° oven for 20 to 25 minutes or until heated through and slightly crisp on top. **Makes 6 servings.**

Corn Bread: In a medium bowl, whisk together 1½ cups cornmeal, ¾ cup all-purpose flour, 1 tablespoon baking powder and ½ teaspoon salt. Using your fingers, rub ¼ cup butter (cut into cubes) into flour mixture until it resembles coarse crumbs. (Or use a pastry blender.) Add ¾ cup buttermilk and 1 egg. Stir with a fork until dough comes together, adding drizzles of buttermilk, if necessary, to moisten. On a baking sheet lined with parchment paper, press dough to ½-inch thickness. (Don't worry about the shape.) Bake in a 400° oven for 12 to 15 minutes or until golden brown and crisp on the edges. When cool enough to handle, coarsely crumble. Use immediately or chill in an airtight container up to 3 days.

*Tip: Our corn bread is thin and dry so that it can be baked and crumbled right away for dressing. You can substitute 7 cups of any crumbled dried corn bread.

**Make-ahead directions: At this point, refrigerate, covered, up to 12 hours. Remove from refrigerator 45 minutes before baking.

Per serving: 390 cal, 17 g fat, 54 mg chol, 1,101 mg sodium, 53 g carbo, 5 g fiber, 9 g pro.

Braised Cabbage with Spicy Croutons

PREP 10 minutes **COOK** 18 minutes

2 tablespoons olive oil
1 tablespoon butter
⅓ of a 12-ounce baguette, torn into coarse cubes (2 cups)
¼ teaspoon garlic powder
¼ teaspoon crushed red pepper
1 small head green cabbage, cut into 6 wedges
Salt
Ground black pepper
½ cup water
Snipped fresh parsley
Lemon wedges

1. For croutons: In a very large skillet, heat 1 tablespoon olive oil and the butter over medium-high heat. Add bread cubes, garlic powder and crushed red pepper. Cook and stir for 3 to 5 minutes, until golden brown. Remove croutons from skillet with a slotted spoon; place in a single layer on paper towels; cool.

2. Add cabbage to skillet, overlapping wedges if needed. Season with salt and black pepper. Add the water; bring to boiling. Reduce heat and simmer, covered, about 15 minutes or until tender.

3. Place cabbage on platter; drizzle with remaining olive oil. Top with croutons and parsley; serve with lemon wedges. **Makes 6 to 8 servings.**

Per serving: 141 cal, 7 g fat, 5 mg chol, 254 mg sodium, 19 g carbo, 4 g fiber, 4 g pro.

Chocolate, Hazelnut and Maple Bacon Scones

PREP 15 minutes **BAKE** 12 minutes **COOL** 5 minutes

  2 cups all-purpose flour
  ½ cup packed brown sugar
  ¼ cup unsweetened cocoa powder
  2½ teaspoons baking powder
  ½ teaspoon baking soda
  ½ teaspoon salt
  ½ cup cold butter, cut into 8 pieces
  2 eggs
  ½ cup whipping cream
  ½ teaspoon vanilla
  ¾ cup bittersweet or semisweet
      chocolate pieces
  ½ cup coarsely chopped toasted hazelnuts
      (see tip, page 167)
  6 slices thick-sliced maple-flavor bacon,
      crisp-cooked, drained and crumbled
      Whipping cream (optional)
      Coarse sugar (optional)

1. In a large bowl, stir together flour, brown sugar, cocoa powder, baking powder, baking soda and salt. Using a pastry blender or your fingertips, cut or rub in the cold butter until mixture resembles coarse crumbs. Make a well in the center of flour mixture; set aside.

2. In a small bowl, stir together eggs, the ½ cup whipping cream and the vanilla. Add egg mixture to flour mixture. Add chocolate pieces, hazelnuts and bacon. Using a fork, stir just until moistened.

3. Turn dough out onto a lightly floured surface. Gently knead dough for 10 to 12 strokes or until dough is nearly smooth. (Handle as little as possible to keep it light.) With a floured knife, cut dough in half. Lightly roll or pat each dough half into a 5½-inch circle, about 1 inch thick. Cut each round into six wedges and brush excess flour off tops.

4. Place wedges 1 inch apart on a baking sheet lined with parchment paper or an ungreased baking sheet. If you like, brush scones with additional whipping cream and sprinkle with coarse sugar.

5. Bake in a 425° oven for 12 to 14 minutes or until bottoms are lightly browned. Remove scones from baking sheet. Cool on a wire rack for 5 minutes. Serve warm. **Makes 12 scones.**

Per scone: 353 cal, 23 g fat, 73 mg chol, 498 mg sodium, 33 g carbo, 2 g fiber, 8 g pro.

Candy Cane Popcorn Mix

PREP 30 minutes **STAND** 1 hour

  7 cups unsalted popped popcorn
  3 cups small pretzel twists
  2 cups lightly salted dry-roasted cashews or
      honey-roasted peanuts
  1¼ pounds vanilla-flavor candy coating,
      coarsely chopped
  1 cup very finely crushed candy canes or
      other hard peppermint candies

1. In a shallow roasting pan, combine popcorn, pretzels and cashews; set aside.

2. In a heavy medium saucepan, melt candy coating over low heat, stirring constantly, until smooth. Remove from heat. Stir in ½ cup of the crushed candy.

3. Pour candy coating mixture over popcorn mixture. Stir gently to coat. Spread onto a large piece of foil or parchment paper. Sprinkle with the remaining ½ cup crushed candy. Cool and break into pieces. Store in an airtight container for up to 1 week. **Makes 24 servings.**

Per serving: 259 cal, 13 g fat, 0 mg chol, 146 mg sodium, 33 g carbo, 1 g fiber, 3 g pro.

The irresistible flavor combination of sweet and salty gets a dash of peppermint in this pretty holiday popcorn mix.

CANDY CANE
POPCORN MIX

Cross-country skiers can choose from miles of well-groomed trails—some of which have lights for night skiing—at Crystal Mountain Resort and Spa in Thompsonville, Michigan. Crystal Mountain exudes tranquillity, whether visitors ski downhill, cross-country, or not at all.

Gingerbread Trifle

The gingerbread in this trifle has dense texture and peppery ginger flavor. About two-thirds of the cake is used for the trifle. Save the rest for snacking or cut it into cubes to toast and serve with ice cream.

PREP 50 minutes **BAKE** 25 minutes **CHILL** 2 hours

2 cups flour
1½ teaspoons baking soda
1 tablespoon ground ginger
1 teaspoon ground cinnamon
½ teaspoon salt
½ cup unsalted butter
1 cup molasses
¼ cup packed brown sugar
¾ cup very hot water
2 eggs
4 egg yolks
2 eggs
½ cup granulated sugar
½ cup lemon juice
2 ounces white chocolate, chopped
1 cup whipping cream
Cranberry Compote (recipe follows)
Slivered candied ginger

1. For gingerbread: Grease a 9x9x2-inch square pan, then line bottom with parchment paper. In a medium bowl, sift together flour, baking soda, ginger, cinnamon and salt; set aside. In a small saucepan, heat butter, molasses, brown sugar and the ¾ cup very hot water until hot, stirring, until butter and brown sugar are melted. In a large bowl, whisk the 2 eggs until blended. Slowly whisk in molasses mixture. Stir in dry ingredients. Pour batter into prepared pan. Bake in a 350° oven about 25 minutes, until a wooden toothpick inserted near center comes out clean.

2. Cool gingerbread in pan. Remove from pan. Tear two-thirds of the cake into pieces (about 7 cups). Set aside until ready to assemble trifle.

3. For cream filling: In a bowl, whisk together egg yolks, 2 whole eggs, granulated sugar and lemon juice. Transfer to a heavy medium-size saucepan. Cook over medium-low heat, stirring constantly with a wooden spoon until thick. If mixture becomes lumpy, whisk until smooth. Remove from heat. Whisk in white chocolate until smooth. Strain into bowl. Cover with plastic wrap directly on surface. Refrigerate until cold.

4. Meanwhile, whip cream until soft peaks form (remove, cover and chill ½ cup whipped cream for topper). Fold remaining whipped cream into cream filling. Refrigerate until ready to assemble trifle.

5. To assemble trifle: In a 7- to 9-inch trifle bowl or container, spoon half the cream filling in an even layer. Evenly top with gingerbread pieces. Spoon the remaining cream filling on gingerbread. Spoon Cranberry Compote over gingerbread layer, spreading evenly. Top with reserved whipped cream and slivered candied ginger. **Makes 10 to 12 servings.**

Cranberry Compote: In a medium saucepan, combine one 12-ounce package cranberries, ½ cup water and ⅓ to ½ cup granulated sugar. Cook over medium heat, stirring occasionally, until cranberries are soft, about 10 minutes. Cool completely. Stir in 1½ cups sliced strawberries.

Per serving: 452 cal, 21 g fat, 205 mg chol, 257 mg sodium, 63 g carbo, 3 g fiber, 6 g pro.

Chocolate Cream Pie

You can use either regular or Dutch-process cocoa in this indulgent chocolate pie. Regular cocoa powder will give you a more intense chocolate taste. Dutch-process cocoa is milder in flavor.

PREP 45 minutes **BAKE** 18 minutes **CHILL** 4 hours

1⅓ cups all-purpose flour
2 tablespoons unsweetened cocoa powder
4½ teaspoons granulated sugar
¼ teaspoon salt
½ cup shortening, chilled and cut up
3 to 4 tablespoons ice water
1 cup chopped semisweet chocolate (6 ounces)
2 tablespoons butter
3 cups whole milk
⅔ cup granulated sugar
4 egg yolks
3 tablespoons cornstarch
2 tablespoons unsweetened cocoa powder
1 teaspoon vanilla
¾ cup whipping cream
2 tablespoons sour cream
1 tablespoon powdered sugar
Chocolate curls or grated semisweet chocolate

1. In a medium bowl, combine flour, 2 tablespoons cocoa, 4½ teaspoons sugar and the salt. Using a pastry blender, cut shortening into flour mixture until it resembles coarse crumbs.

2. Sprinkle 1 tablespoon ice water over part of the mixture. Gently toss with a fork. Continue adding water, 1 tablespoon at a time, until all dough is moistened. Form dough into a ball. On a lightly floured surface, press into a disk, then roll into a 12-inch circle. Ease circle into a 9-inch pie plate. Trim pastry to ½ inch beyond edge of pie plate. Fold under extra crust and crimp as desired.

3. Prick bottom and sides of pastry with a fork. Line crust with a double layer of foil. Bake in a 425° oven for 10 minutes. Remove foil and bake for 8 minutes more or until set and dry. Remove from oven and cool completely.

4. Place chopped chocolate and butter in a medium bowl; set aside. Heat milk in a large heavy saucepan over medium heat until steam rises from surface (do not let boil). Meanwhile, in a medium bowl, whisk together ⅔ cup granulated sugar, the yolks, cornstarch and 2 tablespoons cocoa powder (mixture will be thick).

5. Slowly whisk 2 cups of hot milk into egg mixture. Add egg mixture to saucepan. Cook and stir until mixture comes to a boil. Cook for 30 seconds more. Pour over chopped chocolate and butter. Let stand for 3 minutes. Add vanilla; whisk until chocolate and butter are melted and mixture is smooth.

6. Pour into cooled crust. Cover pie with plastic wrap and refrigerate for at least 4 hours or overnight until set.

7. To serve, in a large mixing bowl, beat whipping cream, sour cream and powdered sugar on medium speed just until stiff peaks form. Spread over pie; top with chocolate curls. **Makes 8 servings.**

Per serving: 589 cal, 38 g fat, 141 mg chol, 154 mg sodium, 58 g carbo, 3 g fiber, 9 g pro.

Decadent Chocolate-Peanut Butter Cheesecake

PREP 40 minutes **BAKE** 45 minutes
COOL 45 minutes **CHILL** 4 hours
STAND 15 minutes

Chocolate Crumb Crust (recipe follows)
2 8-ounce packages cream cheese, softened
1 cup creamy peanut butter
¼ cup sugar
3 eggs, lightly beaten
1½ cups semisweet chocolate pieces
2 tablespoons milk
½ teaspoon vanilla

1. Prepare Chocolate Crumb Crust; set aside. In mixing bowl, beat one package cream cheese with an electric mixer until smooth. Beat in peanut butter and ¼ cup sugar. Fold in one egg; set aside.

2. In saucepan, stir chocolate over low heat until melted. Remove from heat. Cube remaining cream cheese; stir into chocolate. Stir in milk and vanilla. Fold in 2 eggs. Spread half the chocolate mixture in crust. Spread all the peanut butter mixture over layer. Evenly spread remaining chocolate mixture over peanut butter layer.

3. Bake in a 300° oven about 45 minutes or until top is set when lightly shaken. Cool in pan on rack 15 minutes. Use small sharp knife to loosen crust from sides; cool 30 minutes. Remove sides of pan; cool completely on rack. Cover; chill 4 hours. Let stand at room temperature 15 minutes before serving. **Makes 16 servings.**

Chocolate Crumb Crust: Combine 1½ cups finely crushed chocolate graham cracker squares (18); ½ cup butter, melted; and 2 tablespoons sugar. Press into bottom and 1 inch up sides of a 9-inch springform pan.

Per serving: 404 cal, 31 g fat, 85 mg chol, 233 mg sodium, 26 g carbo, 2 g fiber, 8 g pro.

Triple-Pear Pie with Walnut Crust

PREP 45 minutes **BAKE** 1 hour 20 minutes

⅓ cup walnuts, toasted (see tip, page 39)
2 tablespoons packed brown sugar
1 teaspoon salt
2½ cups all-purpose flour
½ cup cold unsalted butter, cut up
¼ cup shortening, chilled and cut up
⅓ to ½ cup ice water
⅔ cup pear nectar or apple juice
¾ cup chopped dried pears or golden raisins
½ teaspoon ground cardamom
¼ teaspoon freshly ground nutmeg
½ cup packed brown sugar
3 tablespoons all-purpose flour
8 ripe Bosc pears (2⅔ pounds)
1 egg, lightly beaten
2 teaspoons water
Coarse white decorating sugar

1. Place walnuts, 2 tablespoons brown sugar and the salt in bowl of food processor. Cover and pulse until walnuts are finely ground. Add 2½ cups flour and pulse until combined. Add cold butter and shortening; pulse until mixture resembles coarse crumbs. Drizzle the cold water through feed tube while pulsing until mixture just begins to come together (do not overprocess). Mixture should still be slightly crumbly but come together when gently squeezed. Gather dough into a ball, divide it in half and shape each half into a disk. Wrap disks in plastic wrap and chill while preparing pie filling.

2. In a small saucepan, bring pear nectar to a simmer over medium-high heat. Add dried pears, cardamom and nutmeg; remove from heat and set aside.

3. In a large bowl, combine ½ cup brown sugar and 3 tablespoons flour. Peel, core and slice pears ½ inch thick; add to sugar mixture. Toss to coat. Add undrained dried pear mixture and toss to combine.

4. On a lightly floured surface, roll one disk of dough into a 12-inch circle. Ease circle into a 9-inch pie plate, allowing pastry to extend over edge. In a small bowl, combine egg and 2 teaspoons water. Lightly brush pastry with some of the egg mixture. Spoon pear mixture evenly into the pastry-lined pie plate. Trim pastry to edge of pie plate.

5. Roll out remaining pastry to an 11-inch circle. Cut slits in pastry and place over filling. Fold top pastry under bottom pastry and crimp edges to seal. Brush with egg mixture; sprinkle with coarse sugar.

6. Loosely cover pie with foil to prevent overbrowning. Bake in a 375° oven for 50 minutes. Remove foil and bake for 30 to 40 minutes more or until pastry is golden, pears are tender and filling is bubbly (if necessary, cover with foil the last 10 minutes of baking to prevent overbrowning). Cool on a wire rack.
Makes 8 servings.

Per serving: 563 cal, 22 g fat, 54 mg chol, 310 mg sodium, 85 g carbo, 8 g fiber, 7 g pro.

TRIPLE-PEAR PIE
WITH WALNUT CRUST

White Christmas Peppermint Layer Cake

PREP 30 minutes **BAKE** 30 minutes **COOL** 2 hours

2¼ cups cake flour
1 tablespoon baking powder
1¼ cups whole milk
4 egg whites
1 teaspoon vanilla
½ cup (1 stick) butter, softened
1½ cups granulated sugar
¾ cup butter, softened
8 cups powdered sugar
⅓ cup milk
2 teaspoons peppermint extract
Red or pink food coloring
Peppermint sticks, candy canes or other peppermint candies

1. Grease two 8x2-inch round cake pans. Line bottoms of pans with waxed paper; grease paper; lightly dust pans with flour; set aside.

2. In a medium bowl, stir together flour and baking powder; set aside. In another medium bowl, whisk together milk, egg whites and vanilla; set aside.

3. In a large mixing bowl, beat ½ cup butter with an electric mixer on low to medium speed for 30 seconds. Add granulated sugar; beat for 3 minutes on medium speed. Alternately add flour and milk mixtures, beating on low speed after each addition until combined. Beat for 2 minutes on medium speed. Divide the batter between the prepared pans.

4. Bake in a 350° oven for 30 to 35 minutes or until a wooden toothpick inserted near centers comes out clean. Cool in pans on wire racks for 10 minutes. Run a knife around the sides to loosen; remove from pans. Peel off waxed paper. Invert cake layers and cool thoroughly on racks.

5. Meanwhile, prepare frosting. In a very large mixing bowl, beat ¾ cup butter with an electric mixer on medium speed until smooth. Gradually add 2 cups powdered sugar, beating well. Slowly beat in ⅓ cup milk and the peppermint extract. Gradually beat in remaining powdered sugar. If necessary, beat in additional milk, 1 tablespoon at a time, to reach spreading consistency.

6. Transfer 2 cups of the frosting to a medium mixing bowl; tint pale pink.

7. With a long serrated knife, halve each cake horizontally to make a total of four layers. Place one layer, cut side up, on a serving plate. Spread top with ⅔ cup of the pink frosting. Repeat with two more cake layers and pink frosting. Top with the last cake layer, cut side down. Spread white frosting over top and sides. Decorate as desired with crushed or whole peppermint candies. **Makes 12 servings.**

Per serving: 716 cal, 20 g fat, 54 mg chol, 327 mg sodium, 131 g carbo, 0 g fiber, 5 g pro.

Kicked-up snow tickles the cheeks of dogsled riders as a tailwagging team of eight—led by Thor, who has raced in Alaska's Iditarod—pulls the sled through the glistening landscape of Michigan's Crystal Mountain resort.

Cornmeal Pumpkin Cake with Dried Fruit Compote

Riesling-poached fruit and billowy whipped cream crown a dense spice cake inspired by ingredients from the first Thanksgiving.

PREP 1 hour **BAKE** 55 minutes **COOL** 15 minutes **COOK** 20 minutes

1½ cups all-purpose flour
½ cup cornmeal
2 tablespoons unsweetened cocoa powder
1 teaspoon baking powder
1 teaspoon ground cinnamon
½ teaspoon baking soda
½ teaspoon salt
¼ teaspoon ground nutmeg
1½ cups canned pumpkin
3 tablespoons orange juice
2 teaspoons grated fresh ginger
1 teaspoon vanilla
¾ cup butter, softened
1 cup packed brown sugar
½ cup granulated sugar
3 eggs
⅓ cup chopped toasted pecans (see tip, page 39)
Dried Fruit Compote (recipe follows)
Sweetened whipped cream (optional)

1. Grease a 9x2-inch round cake pan and line bottom with parchment paper. Grease and flour the parchment and sides of the pan; set aside.

2. In a medium bowl, whisk together the first eight ingredients (through nutmeg); set aside. In a small bowl, combine pumpkin, orange juice, ginger and vanilla.

3. In a large mixing bowl, beat butter with an electric mixer for 30 seconds or until light and fluffy. Beat in brown sugar and granulated sugar until well blended. Beat in eggs, one at a time, until light and fluffy, scraping bowl occasionally.

4. Alternately add pumpkin mixture and flour mixture to the butter mixture, one-third at a time, stirring after each addition until just blended. (Mixture will look curdled.) Fold in pecans.

5. Spread evenly in prepared pan. Bake in a 350° oven for 55 to 60 minutes or until a toothpick inserted into center comes out clean. Cool in pan 15 minutes. Turn out onto a cooling rack and remove parchment paper. Turn cake right side up on a serving plate. Serve warm or room temperature with Dried Fruit Compote and, if you like, sweetened whipped cream. **Makes 16 servings.**

Dried Fruit Compote: In a medium saucepan, combine 2 cups Riesling wine, 2 cups water and ⅓ cup granulated sugar. Using a 4-inch square of 100%-cotton cheesecloth and kitchen string, make a bag containing 1 cinnamon stick, 1 star anise and 2 cloves. Add spice bag to saucepan. Cook and stir over medium-high heat until mixture comes to boiling. Add 8 Mission figs, quartered lengthwise, and cook for 2 minutes. Add 10 dried apricots, cut into strips, and cook for 2 minutes more. Add ¾ cup dried tart cherries and cook for 1 more minute. Using a slotted spoon, transfer fruit to a bowl. Continue cooking liquid about 12 minutes or until reduced to about 1 cup. Remove spice bag and discard. Pour liquid over fruit. Cool to room temperature before serving. (Compote can be chilled, covered, up to 4 days. Bring to room temperature before serving or, if you like, warm slightly.)

Per serving: 326 cal, 12 g fat, 58 mg chol, 243 mg sodium, 49 g carbo, 3 g fiber, 4 g pro.

Gingered Fruitcake

PREP 25 minutes **BAKE** 40 minutes **COOL** 2 hours

¾ cup pecan halves, toasted (see tip, page 39)
2 cups all-purpose flour
1¼ cups sugar
1 tablespoon baking powder
½ teaspoon salt
½ cup milk
½ cup butter, softened
2 eggs
1 cup dried apples, chopped
⅔ cup dried apricots, chopped (not unsulfured)
2 tablespoons grated fresh ginger
Honey-Bourbon Butter (recipe follows) (optional)

1. Grease and lightly flour a 9-inch springform pan.

2. Place ½ cup of the toasted pecans in a food processor. Cover and process until finely ground; set aside.

3. In a large mixing bowl, combine ground pecans, flour, sugar, baking powder and salt. Add milk, butter and eggs. Beat with an electric mixer on low speed until combined. Beat on medium speed for 1 minute. Fold in dried fruit and ginger. Transfer to prepared pan. Arrange remaining ¼ cup pecans on top of batter.

4. Bake in a 350° oven about 40 minutes or until a wooden toothpick inserted near center comes out clean. Cool in pan on a wire rack 10 minutes. Remove sides of pan; cool completely. Remove bottom of pan.

5. To serve, pour Honey-Bourbon Butter over fruitcake, if you like. **Makes 10 servings.**

Honey-Bourbon Butter: In a small saucepan, melt ¼ cup butter. Add 2 tablespoons bourbon and 1 tablespoon honey. Stir until heated through.

To store: Use bourbon or orange juice to moisten a large piece of 100%-cotton cheesecloth; wrap cake in cheesecloth. Place in a large resealable plastic bag or wrap in plastic wrap. Store in refrigerator up to 1 week.

Per serving: 451 cal, 20 g fat, 75 mg chol, 460 mg sodium, 64 g carbo, 3 g fiber, 6 g pro.

A street vendor at Manistee, Michigan's annual Victorian Christmas celebration offers warm and sweet roasted chestnuts—a true taste of the past.

Toasted Fennel Lemon Cake

We like the sweeter flavor of Meyer lemons in this cake. Look for them in bags at large supermarkets. If you substitute regular lemons, reduce the zest to 2 tablespoons.

PREP 40 minutes **STAND** 30 minutes **BAKE** 55 minutes **COOL** 1 hour

  1 cup butter
  5 eggs
  4 teaspoons fennel seeds
  3 cups all-purpose flour
2½ teaspoons baking powder
  ½ teaspoon salt
  2 cups sugar
  2 teaspoons vanilla
  ⅔ cup buttermilk
  ¼ cup Meyer lemon zest
  ½ cup Meyer lemon juice
  1 cup flaked coconut
  ¼ cup sugar
  2 tablespoons Meyer lemon juice
    Candied lemon slices* (optional)

1. Let butter and eggs stand at room temperature for 30 minutes. Meanwhile, in a small skillet, heat and stir fennel seeds over medium heat about 2 minutes or until fragrant; cool. Lightly crush seeds with a mortar and pestle (if available). Set aside. In a medium bowl, combine flour, baking powder and salt; set aside.

2. In a very large mixing bowl, beat butter on medium to high speed with an electric mixer for 30 seconds. Gradually add the 2 cups sugar, beating about 4 minutes or until light and fluffy. Beat in vanilla. Add eggs, one at a time, beating for 20 to 30 seconds after each addition. Alternately add flour mixture and buttermilk, beating on low to medium speed after each addition just until combined. Stir in fennel seeds, lemon zest, the ½ cup lemon juice and the coconut.

3. Spread batter evenly in a greased and floured 10-inch fluted tube pan. Bake in a 350° oven for 55 to 60 minutes or until a wooden toothpick inserted near the center comes out clean and the top springs back when lightly touched. Cool in pan on a wire rack for 10 minutes.

4. Meanwhile, in a small saucepan, stir the ¼ cup sugar and the 2 tablespoons lemon juice over medium heat until sugar is dissolved. Invert cake onto a wire rack set over a shallow baking pan. Poke holes into top of cake using a wooden toothpick or skewer. Spoon glaze over cake. Cool thoroughly. If you like, garnish with candied lemon slices. **Makes 12 servings.**

*Tip: For candied lemon slices: In a large skillet, combine ¾ cup sugar and ¼ cup water; bring to boiling. Add 2 thinly sliced lemons. Simmer, uncovered, for 1 to 2 minutes or until slices are just softened. Transfer to a wire rack to cool.

Per serving: 470 cal, 20 g fat, 119 mg chol, 398 mg sodium, 68 g carbo, 2 g fiber, 7 g pro.

Add a touch of bright sunshine to foods in winter with a squeeze of citrus.

Peppermint Sugar Cookies

Swirls or candy canes? The choice is yours! For a deep red tint, use gel paste food coloring, available at crafts stores.

PREP 40 minutes **BAKE** 6 or 9 minutes per batch

  2 cups all-purpose flour
  ½ teaspoon baking powder
  ¼ teaspoon salt
  10 tablespoons butter, softened
  1 cup sugar
  1 egg
  1 egg yolk
  ¾ teaspoon peppermint extract
    Red gel paste food coloring
    Red decorating sugar (optional)

1. In a medium bowl, stir together flour, baking powder and salt; set aside.

2. In a large mixing bowl, beat butter with an electric mixer on medium speed for 30 seconds. Add sugar; beat for 2 minutes on medium speed or until mixture is light and fluffy, scraping sides of bowl occasionally. Add egg and egg yolk; beat for 2 minutes on medium speed. Beat in peppermint extract. Gradually add flour mixture, beating on low speed until just combined.

3. Divide dough in half. Knead about ½ teaspoon gel paste food coloring into half of the dough. Leave remaining dough plain. If necessary, wrap and chill dough about 1 hour or until easy to handle.

4. Make desired shape:

Swirls: Divide each red and plain dough portion in half for a total of four portions. Roll a red portion into an 8x6-inch rectangle on waxed paper. Roll a plain portion into an 8x6-inch rectangle on waxed paper. Use the waxed paper and your hand to carefully invert the red rectangle onto the plain rectangle; remove top waxed paper. Starting from a long side, roll up dough using the waxed paper to lift and guide it. Pinch edges to seal; wrap in plastic wrap. Repeat with remaining red and plain doughs. Chill rolls 1 to 2 hours or until firm enough to slice. Unwrap rolls; reshape, if necessary. If you like, roll dough rolls in red decorating sugar. Using a sharp, thin-bladed knife, slice rolls into ¼-inch-thick rounds. Rotate roll while cutting to prevent flattening.

Candy canes: For each cookie, on a lightly floured surface, shape a ½-inch ball of plain dough into a 5-inch rope. Repeat with a ½-inch ball of red dough. Place ropes side by side and twist together. Form into a cane shape.

5. Place cookies 2 inches apart on ungreased cookie sheets. Bake in a 350° oven for 9 to 10 minutes for swirls, 6 to 8 minutes for candy canes or until edges are set. Cool on cookie sheets on wire rack for 1 minute. Transfer cookies to wire racks; cool. (Cool baking sheets between batches.) **Makes about 60 swirls or 52 candy canes.**

Per swirl cookie: 55 cal, 2 g fat, 13 mg chol, 37 mg sodium, 8 g carbo, 0 g fiber, 1 g pro.

Lemon-Vanilla Ornament Cookies

Whether you hang these sugar cookies on a decorative tree or share them at a cookie exchange, these cutouts hold their shape beautifully. It's a great recipe to have in your repertoire.

PREP 1 hour **CHILL** 1 hour **BAKE** 8 minutes per batch **STAND** 5 minutes

- 1 cup unsalted butter, softened
- 1 cup powdered sugar
- 1 egg
- 2½ teaspoons vanilla bean paste or vanilla extract
- 1 teaspoon salt
- 1 teaspoon lemon zest
- 2½ cups all-purpose flour
- 4 cups powdered sugar
- 5 tablespoons water
- 2 tablespoons meringue powder
- Gel paste food coloring

1. For cookies: In a large mixing bowl, beat butter with an electric mixer on medium to high speed for 30 seconds. Add 1 cup powdered sugar and beat until combined. Beat in egg, vanilla bean paste, salt and lemon zest until combined. Beat in as much flour as you can with the mixer. Stir in remaining flour. Wrap in plastic wrap and chill 1 to 2 hours or until easy to handle.

2. On a lightly floured surface, roll dough to ¼-inch thickness. Cut dough using 2- to 3-inch fluted round cutters. Use a drinking straw to cut holes near the top of each round for hanging. Transfer rounds to cookie sheets lined with parchment paper. Bake in a 375° oven 8 to 10 minutes, rotating sheets halfway, until set but not browned. Cool on cookie sheets 5 minutes. If needed, use the straw to recut holes while warm. Transfer to wire racks to cool completely.

3. For Royal Icing: In a stand mixer fitted with a paddle attachment, combine 4 cups powdered sugar, the water and meringue powder. Beat on low to medium speed 7 to 10 minutes or until stiff and no longer shiny. Tint icing with food coloring. Decorate cookies as desired.* **Makes 20 cookies.**

*Tip: You can spoon or brush Royal Icing onto cookies, but for the cleanest look, try the flooding technique. Using a piping bag fitted with a narrow tip, pipe a rim around the edge and the hanging hole. (If icing is too thick, stir in water ¼ teaspoon at a time. If it is too thin, stir in powdered sugar.) Let stand until set. Using icing that has been thinned until it drips off a spoon, flood the center of the cookie. (A squeeze bottle or paintbrush works great for flooding. Use a toothpick to spread icing into corners.) Let set again before piping decorations over the base coat. Keep extra icing covered so it doesn't harden.

Per 3-inch cookie: 260 cal, 10 g fat, 34 mg chol, 122 mg sodium, 42 g carbo, 0 g fiber, 2 g pro.

Spiced Chocolate-Pistachio Cookies

PREP 25 minutes
CHILL 1 hour **BAKE** 10 minutes per batch
STAND 2 minutes

- ¾ cup butter, softened
- 1⅓ cups all-purpose flour
- ½ cup packed brown sugar
- ¼ cup unsweetened cocoa powder
- ½ teaspoon chili powder
- ½ teaspoon ground cinnamon
- ¾ cup miniature semisweet chocolate pieces
- ½ cup semisweet chocolate pieces
- 1 teaspoon shortening
- ½ cup finely chopped pistachio nuts

1. In a large mixing bowl, beat butter on medium to high speed for 30 seconds. Add half of the flour, the brown sugar, cocoa powder and spices. Beat until combined. Stir in the remaining flour. Stir in the ¾ cup chocolate pieces. Wrap and chill dough for 1 to 2 hours, until easy to handle.

2. On a lightly floured surface, roll dough ¼ inch thick. Cut cookies with a 2½- to 3½-inch cutter. Reroll as necessary. Place 2 inches apart on ungreased cookie sheets.

3. Bake in a 325° oven for 10 to 12 minutes or until edges are set and tops look dry. Let stand on cookie sheets for 2 minutes before transferring to wire racks to cool.

4. In a small saucepan, melt the ½ cup chocolate pieces and the shortening over low heat, stirring occasionally.

5. Set wire rack over waxed paper. Dip edges of cookies or one half of each cookie in melted chocolate. (Or drizzle chocolate over the cookie.) Let excess chocolate drip off; roll edges in pistachios or sprinkle pistachios over chocolate. Leave cookies on racks until chocolate sets. **Makes 24 cookies.**

Per cookie: 148 cal, 9 g fat, 15 mg chol, 53 mg sodium, 16 g carbo, 1 g fiber, 2 g pro.

Salty Caramel and Pecan Oatmeal Cookies

Caramel bits give these cookies great flavor and chewy texture. Some supermarkets carry them, and they're widely available online. Take care to follow recipe directions when baking; caramel bits melt quickly.

PREP 30 minutes
BAKE 11 minutes per batch **COOL** 3 minutes

1 cup butter, softened
1 cup granulated sugar
1 cup packed dark brown sugar
1 teaspoon salt
½ teaspoon baking soda
1 teaspoon baking powder
1 teaspoon ground cinnamon
2 eggs
2 teaspoons vanilla
1½ cups all-purpose flour
3 cups rolled oats
1 11-ounce package caramel baking bits
1 cup pecans, toasted (see tip, page 39) and coarsely chopped
Coarse sea salt

1. In a large mixing bowl, beat butter on medium to high speed for 30 seconds. Add the sugars, 1 teaspoon salt, the baking soda, baking powder and cinnamon. Beat until combined, scraping sides of bowl. Beat in eggs and vanilla. Beat in as much of the flour as you can with the electric mixer, then stir in the remaining flour. Stir in oats, caramel baking bits and pecans.

2. Drop 1½-inch mounds of dough 2 inches apart onto cookie sheets lined with parchment paper. Sprinkle with sea salt.

3. Bake in a 350° oven for 11 to 12 minutes, until edges are light brown. (Cookies will look undercooked.) Cool on cookie sheets for 3 to 4 minutes. Transfer to a wire rack; cool. **Makes 48 cookies.**

Per cookie: 145 cal, 7 g fat, 18 mg chol, 421 mg sodium, 21 g carbo, 1 g fiber, 2 g pro.

Eggnog Cheesecake Bars

PREP 25 minutes **BAKE** 33 minutes
COOL 1 hour **CHILL** 4 hours

  1 cup graham cracker crumbs
  3 tablespoons sugar
  ¼ teaspoon ground ginger
  ¼ teaspoon ground cinnamon
  ¼ teaspoon ground nutmeg
  3 tablespoons unsalted butter, melted
  12 ounces cream cheese, softened
  ⅓ cup sugar
  1 egg
  ¾ cup eggnog
  1 tablespoon bourbon (optional)
  Graham cracker crumbs and/or
    crystallized ginger (optional)

1. For crust: In a medium bowl, combine graham cracker crumbs, 3 tablespoons sugar, the ginger, cinnamon and nutmeg. Mix in the melted butter with a fork. Transfer crumb mixture to an 8x8x2-inch baking pan lined with foil or parchment paper. Press flat and even. Bake in a 375° oven for 5 minutes. Remove from oven; reduce oven temperature to 325°.

2. For filling: In a large mixing bowl, beat the cream cheese on medium-high speed until smooth, about 1 minute. Add ⅓ cup sugar; beat 1 minute more. Add egg; beat until smooth. Add eggnog and, if you like, bourbon. Beat on medium speed 1 minute more, until mixture is light and smooth.

3. Pour filling over crust in pan. Bake for 28 to 30 minutes or until center is just set. Cool in pan on wire rack for 1 hour. Refrigerate, covered, at least 4 hours before serving. If you like, garnish with graham cracker crumbs and/or chopped crystallized ginger. **Makes 16 bars.**

Per bar: 168 cal, 11 g fat, 48 mg chol, 119 mg sodium, 14 g carbo, O g fiber, 3 g pro.

Cherry Hazelnut Fudge

PREP 20 minutes **BAKE** 20 minutes
COOK 12 minutes **CHILL** 3 hours

  ½ cup hazelnuts
    Butter
  1 14-ounce can sweetened condensed milk
  1 teaspoon vanilla
  8 ounces bittersweet chocolate,
    finely chopped
  1 cup chocolate-hazelnut spread, such
    as Nutella
  3 tablespoons unsalted butter, softened
  ½ teaspoon coarse sea salt flakes, plus more
    for sprinkling
  ½ cup dried cherries, coarsely chopped

1. Place hazelnuts in a 15x10x1-inch baking pan. Bake in a 250° oven for 20 minutes or until lightly toasted and the skins have cracked. Roll them gently in a kitchen towel to remove skins. Chop coarsely.

2. Line an 8x8x2-inch baking pan with foil; butter the foil lightly; set aside. Set a heatproof bowl on a pot with a few inches of gently simmering water. In the bowl, place sweetened condensed milk, vanilla, chocolate, chocolate-hazelnut spread, 3 tablespoons butter and ½ teaspoon salt. Heat, stirring occasionally, until the mixture is melted and smooth.

3. Remove bowl from heat. Fold hazelnuts and cherries into chocolate mixture. Spread in prepared pan. Cool a few minutes; sprinkle lightly with additional sea salt. Cover; chill until firm, 3 to 4 hours.

4. Use the foil to lift fudge from the pan. Slice into 1-inch squares. Store in an airtight container. **Makes 64 pieces.**

Per 1-inch piece: 77 cal, 4 g fat, 4 mg chol, 47 mg sodium, 9 g carbo, 1 g fiber, 1 g pro.

Raspberry Truffles

A pretty box or plateful of these rich treats makes a lovely hostess gift.

PREP 25 minutes **STAND** 5 minutes
CHILL 2 hours

  8 ounces bittersweet chocolate, finely
    chopped
  ½ cup whipping cream
  3 to 4 tablespoons good-quality
    raspberry preserves
  2 tablespoons unsweetened Dutch-process
    cocoa powder
  2 tablespoons powdered sugar

1. Place chocolate in a heatproof bowl. In a small saucepan, bring whipping cream to a simmer. Pour cream over chocolate and let stand for 5 minutes. Whisk until smooth. Whisk in raspberry preserves. Chill, covered, for 2 hours or until firm enough to scoop.

2. In a small bowl, stir together cocoa powder and powdered sugar. Using a small scoop or measuring spoon, roll chocolate mixture into 1-inch balls. Roll in cocoa powder mixture to coat. Chill until ready to serve. **Makes 28 truffles.**

Per truffle: 64 cal, 5 g fat, 6 mg chol, 3 mg sodium, 7 g carbo, 1 g fiber, 1 g pro.

RASPBERRY
TRUFFLES

METRIC INFORMATION

The charts on this page provide a guide for converting measurements from the U.S. customary system, which is used throughout this book, to the metric system.

PRODUCT DIFFERENCES

Most of the ingredients called for in the recipes in this book are available in most countries. However, some are known by different names. Here are some common American ingredients and their possible counterparts:

- Sugar (white) is granulated, fine granulated or castor sugar.
- Confectioners' sugar is icing sugar.
- All-purpose flour is enriched, bleached or unbleached white household flour. When self-rising flour is used in place of all-purpose flour in a recipe that calls for leavening, omit the leavening agent (baking soda or baking powder) and salt.
- Light-color corn syrup is golden syrup.
- Cornstarch is cornflour.
- Baking soda is bicarbonate of soda.
- Vanilla or vanilla extract is vanilla essence.
- Green, red or yellow sweet peppers are capsicums or bell peppers.
- Golden raisins are sultanas.

VOLUME AND WEIGHT

The United States traditionally uses cup measures for liquid and solid ingredients. The chart, top right, shows the approximate imperial and metric equivalents. If you are accustomed to weighing solid ingredients, the following approximate equivalents will be helpful.

- 1 cup butter, castor sugar or rice = 8 ounces = ½ pound = 250 grams
- 1 cup flour = 4 ounces = ¼ pound = 125 grams
- 1 cup icing sugar = 5 ounces = 150 grams

Canadian and U.S. volume for a cup measure is 8 fluid ounces (237 ml), but the standard metric equivalent is 250 ml. One British imperial cup is 10 fluid ounces.

In Australia, 1 tablespoon equals 20 ml, and there are 4 teaspoons in the Australian tablespoon.

Spoon measures are used for smaller amounts of ingredients. Although the size of the tablespoon varies slightly in different countries, for practical purposes and for recipes in this book, a straight substitution is all that's necessary. Measurements made using cups or spoons always should be level unless stated otherwise.

COMMON WEIGHT RANGE REPLACEMENTS

Imperial / U.S.	Metric
½ ounce	15 g
1 ounce	25 g or 30 g
4 ounces (¼ pound)	115 g or 125 g
8 ounces (½ pound)	225 g or 250 g
16 ounces (1 pound)	450 g or 500 g
1¼ pounds	625 g
1½ pounds	750 g
2 pounds or 2¼ pounds	1,000 g or 1 Kg

OVEN TEMPERATURE EQUIVALENTS

Fahrenheit Setting	Celsius Setting*	Gas Setting
300°F	150°C	Gas Mark 2 (very low)
325°F	160°C	Gas Mark 3 (low)
350°F	180°C	Gas Mark 4 (moderate)
375°F	190°C	Gas Mark 5 (moderate)
400°F	200°C	Gas Mark 6 (hot)
425°F	220°C	Gas Mark 7 (hot)
450°F	230°C	Gas Mark 8 (very hot)
475°F	240°C	Gas Mark 9 (very hot)
500°F	260°C	Gas Mark 10 (extremely hot)
Broil	Broil	Grill

*Electric and gas ovens may be calibrated using celsius. However, for an electric oven, increase celsius setting 10 to 20 degrees when cooking above 160°C. For convection or forced air ovens (gas or electric) lower the temperature setting 25°F/10°C when cooking at all heat levels.

BAKING PAN SIZES

Imperial / U.S.	Metric
9x1½-inch round cake pan	22- or 23x4-cm (1.5 L)
9x1½-inch pie plate	22- or 23x4-cm (1 L)
8x8x2-inch square cake pan	20x5-cm (2 L)
9x9x2-inch square cake pan	22- or 23x4.5-cm (2.5 L)
11x7x1½-inch baking pan	28x17x4-cm (2 L)
2-quart rectangular baking pan	30x19x4.5-cm (3 L)
13x9x2-inch baking pan	34x22x4.5-cm (3.5 L)
15x10x1-inch jelly roll pan	40x25x2-cm
9x5x3-inch loaf pan	23x13x8-cm (2 L)
2-quart casserole	2 L

U.S. / STANDARD METRIC EQUIVALENTS

⅛ teaspoon = 0.5 ml	⅓ cup = 3 fluid ounces = 75 ml
¼ teaspoon = 1 ml	½ cup = 4 fluid ounces = 125 ml
½ teaspoon = 2 ml	⅔ cup = 5 fluid ounces = 150 ml
1 teaspoon = 5 ml	¾ cup = 6 fluid ounces = 175 ml
1 tablespoon = 15 ml	1 cup = 8 fluid ounces = 250 ml
2 tablespoons = 25 ml	2 cups = 1 pint = 500 ml
¼ cup = 2 fluid ounces = 50 ml	1 quart = 1 litre